My Wi

MW00967046

My Wife Has All the Answers

Thanks for all
you do.

Best wishes,

Mike Parker

12/19/07

Mike Parker

Imprint Books, Inc.
Charleston, SC

ISBN 1-59109-347-3

My Wife Has All the Answers

TABLE OF CONTENTS

ACKNOWLEDGEMENTS

The material in this book first appeared in The Free Press of Kinston, NC. I am grateful to the editors and staff of The Free Press. They apprenticed me to this craft – at their peril – and have encouraged me in this project. My association with The Free Press dates back to 1980. Special thanks to Mike Kohler and the late Ken Hamrick, two of the finest editors I've ever known.

I appreciate the willingness of Levin K. Jones, my assistant principal at Dobbs Youth Development Center; my son, Michael; and my daughter, Rachel, to read the manuscript, offer suggestions for improvement, and catch some of the errors. Thanks to them, this book is as good as it is. The flaws still present are my responsibility.

I would also like to thank Isaac Hines; his wife, Linda; and their daughter, Susan, for shooting the cover photography. They are dear friends who always offer a kind word and stand ready to help. The cover photos are courtesy of Photographic Expressions by Isaac, their family business.

Mary Edwards was a driving force behind this book. She urged me to publish a collection of my columns and prodded me to start this project. She consistently offered encouragement and suggestions. Thank you, Mary.

Finally, I would like to express gratitude to my wife, Sandra. She is my first editor, my greatest cheerleader, and the source of much of my inspiration and material. After all, without her, this book would be untitled. Some of you may be wondering if she really has all the answers. If you doubt me, just ask her.

INTRODUCTION

When Mary Edwards encouraged me to publish a collection of my newspaper columns about three years ago, I was skeptical. However, her relentless attempts to convince me to publish them eventually wore me down. I first started this process figuring I would pick out columns already stored on my computer, string them together in some sort of order, and be done with it. What I have learned is that newspaper writing is a different animal than book preparation. I write a weekly column for The Free Press of Kinston, NC. I try to produce solid work for my readers, but I have a deadline to meet. Each column is as good as I can make it by the time it is due. Deadline writing leaves little opportunity for reflective fine-tuning.

A book has different standards. I owe you, my readers, the best I can produce. Some of you may read this collection and hope that if it represents my best work, you never encounter the worst. Others of you will read more kindly, and the chords of human experience that vibrated in me as I wrote will resonate within you as you read.

Please keep in mind that these columns were never written to fit together as a whole. In fact, they were written over an eight-year period. Some pieces I have included date from the mid-1980s. As you read from page to page, though, I hope you will find coherence.

But what I most hope is that as you read, the experiences I share will ring true with those of your own life. If what you read brings a smile or a sigh or a tear, if you hug your children or grandchildren a little tighter, if you hold your husband's or wife's hand a little more often, or if you search for the good and lovely and true in this world that bombards us with the bad, ugly and false, then our mutual investment of time and energy will return rich dividends to both of us.

If not, blame Mary.

Mike Parker
Kinston, NC
June 2002

To my wife, Sandra, and my parents, Henry and Irene Parker

CHAPTER ONE

'DON'T CONFUSE ME WITH THE FACTS'

Riding the temperature roller-coaster

My wife Sandra and I sat in a doctor's office as he finished questioning her about her medical history.

"Are there any other problems you would like to discuss?" he asked. After a brief silence, I cleared my throat.

"Well, yeah, doctor. I do have one other thing I'd like to bring up," I started cautiously, stealing a glance toward Sandra. "Can you—like—replace her thermostat? I mean, her temperature control system doesn't seem to be working at all."

The doctor looked stunned, started to speak, stopped, and then suddenly smiled.

"Mr. Parker, I believe that problem is beyond my medical expertise."

"Can you make a referral then?" I pleaded. He just shook his head—no.

A disservice we older men routinely commit against our younger counterparts is failing to warn them of a woman's inability to be comfortable at any given temperature. Sandra vows her pendulum swings between freezing and incinerating is a new phenomenon. Of course, selective memory is another problem she experiences at times.

"Don't you remember the little song the girls used to sing nearly every time we took a trip anywhere?" I asked. She sheepishly shook her head no, indicating a willful memory lapse. I decided to chant it for her.

"Honey, cut the heater up. Honey, I'm cold. Honey, cut the heater down—a little bit—whoa!" I sang in my best falsetto. Now, contrary to her claims, I never wrote, co-wrote, or encouraged the girls to sing that ditty. Sandra's constant demands at temperature adjustment made such an impression on my girls that these words sprang from the mouths of babes without any coaxing on my part.

But, I must admit, the problem has grown worse. Her sudden and frequent temperature shifts that once took minutes now take just a few seconds. Can you imagine how aggravating it is to drive down the road constantly adjusting fan speed and air-conditioning settings? She tries to keep her temperature changes to herself, but somehow, I always catch on.

For instance, if I am riding down the road with the AC on "2" and see her grab a sweater and clutch it just beneath her chin, then I suspect a cold front has moved into her personal weather system. When, in the next 10 seconds, she tosses the sweater off her like a leper's rag and begins pointing every available air vent directly on her, then summer has arrived in Sandra-land.

"Honey, did you cut the air conditioner down?" is the signal for a full-scale assault on the heat. Fan speed to warp factor four, Mr. Sulu. AC setting to maximum. I reach to cut off my vent to send even more frigid air her way. I hear Scotty call from engineering, "She canna take much more, Captain." Then just as suddenly, my poor wife turns blue, snatches her sweater and pulls it to her chin as I begin reversing dials faster than a nuclear engineer with a core meltdown message.

"I'll probably be the only guy in the world who trades in a car with defective comfort controls," I say, as she reaches for my sweater in the back seat—the one I keep for just such an emergency.

Her latest surprises are "flashes." She can flash at any time—without warning. Her little pale face suddenly turns bright red, and her blanket (she was freezing just a minute ago) begins to fly away in all directions. At peak flash, she could serve as a role model for Rudolph and his famous nose.

So, young men, beware. While you bask in the land of nearly constant temperature comfort, your significant other is experiencing temperatures that change faster than weather in North Carolina. Enduring these red and blue shifts is just one peril of being a man addicted to love.

"Honey, it's hot," she said as she reviewed this column. "I've got to go find some cool air."

Good luck, my love.

Beware those 'three little words'

Every now and then, my sense of public spirit moves me to share an insight years of marriage have taught me. Most men readily admit that they do not understand women, so whenever I have an epiphany of sorts, I know my duty. Recently I warned younger men about the defective thermostat most women seem to have. Today, a darker secret.

Before Sandra and I married, she impressed me. I had never met an adult human being who ate as little as she did. One of our favorite restaurants during our dating days was The Three Steers Restaurant.

Now, I was raised essentially as a "meat and potatoes" guy. Anything green or leafy made me suspicious. Sandra and I would go the Three Steers and order steaks. During the time we dated, she could never manage to finish more than half her steak. She always asked if I wanted the other half. That offer was music to my ears and endeared her to my gastrointestinal system.

Well, on February 18, 1972, we married. Somehow, during that first week of marriage, her appetite transformed. The next time we went to our restaurant, she not only ate all her steak but also asked for half of mine. What could I do? She had shared so many times, I just didn't have the heart to say no. That salad started to look good after I saw her haul half my steak onto her plate.

"Hungry tonight?" I asked. She just glared. Perhaps she had been suffering loss of appetite from some sort of love sickness that marriage suddenly cured. I have discussed this series of events with my fellow husbands and discovered my situation closely parallels their experiences.

But change in appetite caused by marriage is not the only strange eating habit women have. I guess every man alive with a significant other has experienced this scenario. I go into a restaurant—usually a fast food joint—to grab a quick snack or meal on the run.

"Do you want anything, Honey?" I always ask.

"No," Sandra says demurely. "I'll just eat a bite of yours."

At first I was a fool. I'd order my burger, fries and drink. When I would bring the stuff to the table, I always gave her first option. She would pull the tray over and, while I fumbled for something in my pocket, she'd work her magic by making my food disappear. Of course, she always left two bites of burger, five fries, and two tablespoons of drink.

For years I thought that what drove Sandra's behavior was some sort of weird fluke of luck. For some reason she just didn't realize she was hungry until she saw or smelled my food up close and personal. Young men, I am here to tell you that conclusion is not accurate. Beware those three little words: "Just a bite." They spell hunger—for you.

I again compared notes with fellow hungry husbands and found they had the same "just a bite" stories. But what topped everything was a recent visit to Greenville. As we left the doctor's office, Sandra announced that she needed to eat something.

"What are you in the mood for?" I replied.

"Ham, eggs and a biscuit," she said. For lunch? We reviewed the Greenville locales that might satisfy her desire. We decided on the IHOP. We both ordered—which meant my food was likely safe for a little while. As we were talking, another couple, a little older than us, sat at a nearby table. A waiter approached and took their orders. The woman ordered some dessert concoction. The man ordered a club sandwich.

"Oooh, that sounds good," she said. I saw the poor guy grimace. I knew what was coming next. "When your sandwich comes, I want just a bite." He gulped and nodded obediently, his eyes misting a little.

When the waiter brought the food, he placed in front of the woman an ice cream entree in something that looked like a glass bucket— at least three quarts of ice cream, chocolate syrup, cherries, strawberries and nuts. But before the poor guy could tuck in his napkin, his companion snatched three of the four triangles of club sandwich. Poor guy sat defeated—the victim of three little words: "Just a bite."

Three little words.

What did I do to deserve this?

Saturday afternoon found me in J.C. Penney's— unfortunately, it was not my first shopping trip with my wife Sandra. In fact, I have learned quite a bit about shopping for women's clothes. I have piled up so many hours in shopping with my wife that I must have earned a graduate degree somewhere along the line—a Ph.D. in waiting, fetching, and nodding.

Lesson One: Women's clothes come in a host of sizes. In addition to small, medium, large, and the numbers (2, 4, 6, 8, 10, 12, 14, etc.), a shopper must pay attention to Petite, Miss, Junior, Full Figured, and Plus.

Shopping for a guy's clothes is child's play. If a man can discern whether he needs S, M, L, XL, XXL, XXXL, or WOW, then he is all set. In fairness, we men do have tall sizes, such as XLT—extra large for tall men. With women's clothing, you need something akin to an encyclopedia to ascertain the correct size. Believe me, I have seen college play books easier to memorize.

Lesson Two: Size considerations do not begin to address the mystery of shopping for clothes with a woman. Here's a typical conversation.

"Honey, how do you like this?" I say, holding up a blouse.

"Oh, I can't possibly wear THAT. It will make me look yellow."

"Do what?" I stammer in response.

"Well, that particular shade of brown has too much yellow tint in it, and it just doesn't look good on me."

"Oh," I say, pretending to understand.

"What about this?" I offer.

"No, I am looking for summer colors right now—that a spring color."

"A spring color?"

"Yes. Spring fabrics have more green and the flowers are only buds to suggest the rebirth of life that springtime brings."

"Huh? You mean you have to buy clothes for each season?"

"Oh, sure. After all, you just can't wear certain things after Memorial Day."

I smile and nod, but the screen inside my brain has gone blank.

Here's the man's version of seasonal clothing. Winter: you wear a shirt, pants, shoes, and coat. If breezy, wear a sweater under your coat. Spring: Same as above—just remove coat. Summer: Same as above, except remove sweater and wear a short-sleeved shirt. Fall: Put your sweater on again. Colors? Navy blue, khaki, black, brown—basic and simple, like the mind of a man.

Sooo...back to story at hand. She loads me down with garments. I lumber through the narrow crevices in the women's department, try to avoid knocking over the racks and racks of clothes, and arrive at the dressing room. She takes two or three garments and heads in. I wait...and wait...and wait.

She comes back, wearing the clothes she wore in.

"This blouse was a little tight in places," she says, holding up the object in question. "Go back to the rack and see if you find the next size up."

"Well, if you go to the next size, will the shoulders fit properly?" I ask in perfect innocence. She pauses.

"I'll tell you what," she says, "measure the next size up from here to here," indicating a line on the blouse that goes along the shoulder. "If this line is the same size, bring it back." She snatches up three more garments and disappears into the fitting room.

I walk back to the rack and search for the next size up. I take my time. No hurry. She's in the fitting room. I find the blouse and carefully measure the line along the shoulder. To my amazement, the lines match. I amble across the store to the dressing room again. I wait...and wait...and wait.

She pops out, wearing the same clothes she had on to begin with, grabs the blouse and heads back to the fitting room. I wait...but you get the idea.

She emerges in the same clothes.

"Didn't fit," she said. "Too big." By now I'm wondering if she is really trying on clothes at all. Maybe the store has some sort of refreshment bar in that alleged fitting room.

Finally, the time she allotted for shopping expires and we head out empty-handed.

No wonder she stands in front of a closet crammed with four seasons of clothes and complains, "I don't have anything to wear."

Signs of sad times

On Friday, Sandra and I celebrated our 28th wedding anniversary. I have always thought we were perfectly happy. I hope she would say the same. But then I came into possession of information that has shaken my faith in our relationship to its foundation. Here's my story.

Sandra and I have sort of expanded our anniversary celebration from the traditional "day" to nearly a week. After all, our anniversary is Feb. 18, and Valentine's Day is close by at Feb. 14, so beginning our anniversary celebration on or near Valentine's Day just makes sense—to her.

During a sort of pre-anniversary celebration at the China Garden Thursday night, I noticed the colorful place mat on the table—one of those reddish gold "Chinese Zodiac" sheets. Unlike the western notion of zodiac, each Chinese sign is good for a year and the 12 signs rotate in a 12-year cycle. The Chinese do not recognize Libra and Gemini—or the other constellations western stargazers use to set the limits of their

12 monthly signs.

So as we waited for our ice tea, I looked for Sandra's birth year and discovered that she was born under the Monkey sign. The descriptor read:

"You are very intelligent and are able to influence people."

Boy, that's true, I thought. Sandra is certainly intelligent, and she has influenced me for more than 28 years. Why more than 28? After all, we dated before we got married—and, believe me, she started her version of the "influence" business early on.

"An enthusiastic achiever, you are easily discouraged and confused."

Well, that sort of hits her as well. When enthused, she is a go-getter. When defused, she fits the less-than-flattering descriptors.

"Avoid Tigers. Seek a Dragon or a Rat."

Avoid Tigers? My birth year is 1950. Guess what Chinese zodiac sign I was born under? If you guessed "Tiger," you are right—and you probably didn't need a crystal ball or lifeline to arrive at your final answer.

What are the characteristics of the Tiger?

"Tiger people are aggressive, courageous, candid, and sensitive."

So far, so good. I'd like to think those four adjectives describe me, although I am not sure how "aggressive" I am.

"Look to the Horse and Dog for happiness."

But I already know that I am married to a Monkey. I have no idea which women I've met are Horses or Dogs. In fact, I have heard people use "horsy" to describe a woman, and I didn't think it was flattering at all. And Dog? Some guys I went to school with referred to a few girls as "card-carrying members of the Canine Club." I didn't think these guys were distributing compliments, though.

Next I read: "Beware of the Monkey."

Please notice: Sandra was admonished to "avoid Tigers."

However, I was warned: "Beware!" Remember Julius Caesar? "Beware the ides of March."

So we are assessing our relationship now. Maybe during all

these years we just thought we were happy. Could we have been deceiving ourselves? After all, isn't self-deception one of the strongest deceptions of all?

I am presently researching this new system of mate matching to see how many of my friends have matched as poorly as Sandra and I have. Glenn, a Boar, and Jessica, a Tiger, may not be a perfect zodiacal match, but at least they weren't told to "beware of" or "avoid." Richard is a Snake and Carol is a Horse—not bad. Anita is an Ox and Bo is a Monkey. No problem. Fred is a Boar and Phyllis is an Ox. Not an exact match, but at least no "avoid" or "beware" aimed toward them.

I can tell you this: until Sandra and I get this thing sorted out, we're using another principle that seems to provide for long-term marriages—opposites attract.

Joy of Christmas lights

As we begin winter with its darkness and cold, Christmas seems an oasis in what many of us find a gloomy time of year. Something about bare tree limbs, nights that come early and stay late, and way too much twilight gray just saps my vitality. In contrast, Christmas smiles, Christmas whirls, Christmas sings and shines.

Christmas touches the little child in each of us—a few Scrooges excepted. My wife Sandra has to be one of the biggest kids when it comes to Christmas lights. From Thanksgiving onward, she treats me to excited cries of "Look at those lights!" "Isn't that tree beautiful!" More than a few times I have stomped the brakes when she shouted in glee, "Oh! Look at that!"

After a few yoga exercises to bring my pulse rate below 150, I turned to see what had captivated her attention—and nearly caused my heart attack. What was the inspiration of her exultation? A tree in a window. A series of Christmas lights hanging like icicles from some home's eves. A Santa or a reindeer etched in color and light against the darkness.

But Wednesday night some of our friends took us to what

has to be one of the top light shows in eastern North Carolina—the hayride at Mike's Farm in Back Swamp, NC. Actually, Back Swamp is just a few miles from Beulaville, Richlands, and Chinquapin. Mike's Farm is in the heart of—well—the country. The main entrance is just off Haw Branch Road. No cities, towns or villages in Back Swamp. Mike's Farm features the earth and sky as the good Lord created it. When was the last time you saw the sky without the distraction of mercury lights?

We pulled into the parking lot and entered a country store specializing in baked goods, jellies, jams, and tons of country and Christmas decorations. We paid our fee and waited for our turn on the hay wagon. Before long the guide was loading the next group of holiday gawkers. (If you visit the farm in the next few days, be sure to dress warm. Sorry, all you tenderfoots: no heat on this ride.)

The diesel tractor sputtered, the wagon gave a gentle jolt, and we were on our way as Frank Sinatra crooned Christmas songs. In the early going, we passed some lighted trees. The lights appeared brighter because dense darkness covered the woods and fields. We made a right turn and started heading down the side of a field. No light show there—except the stars in the sky. I picked out the constellations I knew. Orion hangs low in the sky these days, and the stars that form his belt, the "Three Sisters," stand almost perpendicular to the horizon.

We made another right and brushed by some low-hanging trees. I could barely make out the path as he guided our transport through twists and a narrow break in the brush and trees. I could see lights in the background moving closer.

Then the driver wheeled abruptly left, and we entered a world of Christmas lights—a feast for the eyes that gleamed and glimmered against purple black. We passed under arch after arch of lights as we traveled a path between angels, reindeer, a little country church, an old home place—and even a privy for Santa if the old elf needed a pit stop. I marveled that folks would give the time and effort to put up all those lights, to cast spotlights on the church and house and privy, to build shining arches that created a path through the crisp black.

Sandra was a child again, craning her neck to take it all

in, gasping in delight as we passed each new attraction. Some folks from out of state had been chatting energetically until we entered the arches. Their voices fell to a whisper—then stopped in awe. The lights bathed us in the mystery of Christmas and we started singing along with Frank and Tony Bennett, softly at first, but then stronger. We were dreaming of a white Christmas, taking a sleigh ride, jingling bells, and roasting chestnuts over an open fire.

As I saw the lights of the country store come slowly into view, I wondered how a place so wonderful could have escaped my knowledge for so long. Such beauty. Such wonder.

Men and their toys?

Every married man has heard these words issue from his wife dozens of times: "The difference between men and boys is the price of their toys." The first time I bought a VCR, Sandra spouted this maxim. When I bought a $3,600 computer system, she sang the second verse. Buy a new guitar or chromatic tuner? Play it again, Sam.

Recently, I purchased a four-track recorder so my son Michael and I could record music together. Michael makes up songs and guitar leads, but he often forgets them unless he writes them down in tablature. He wanted a way to record his musical musings to avoid losing them. When the four-track arrived, we had a new "toy."

I have pondered this saying through the years. Even before Sandra used the phrase on me, my mom had cast this phrase time and again in my dad's teeth. Do women go to a school to learn this phrase? Is this phrase engraved on their DNA in some sort of amino acid code? Or is making the "toy" allegation learned behavior, passed from mothers to daughters, or from older wives to younger wives?

I have concluded, after being bombarded by the "new toy" claim over and again, that women nearly always use the term "toy" to refer to a piece of equipment they do not know how to use. Take the computer, for instance. Sandra works with a computer on her job, but she only uses it for job-related activities. She understands that the computer on her job is a tool, not a toy.

I have tried to teach her to use my personal computer, but she knows little beyond turning it on. If someone sends her e-mail and depends on her to check it, that e-mail would remain locked in cyberspace until I chanced by to free it from its prison. So, we use the same e-mail address and I print out her e-mail and hand it to her.

She has sat by me when I surfed the Net, but she never climbs aboard. Just after Halloween, Charlie, our nephew, gave us a pumpkin the size of Wyoming. He asked for a single pie in exchange. Sandra cleaned that pumpkin, cut it into strips and used the Salad Master grater (another "toy" I bought years ago) to grate it. She told me a day or so later she needed to use that pumpkin before it went bad, but she lacked a recipe for using fresh pumpkin. (Translation: You need to get up off your posterior and help me make these pies.) Then she took a nap, believing, I guess, that her subconscious would suggest a recipe.

I went on the Net and typed in "pumpkin+pie" and accessed 2,200 pages of recipes for using pumpkin. I read through a hundred or so, looking for ones that used fresh pumpkin. When she awakened, I handed her the best six. We compared the recipes, took parts from each, and created our own. The pies that resulted from that recipe were the best ever—all 14 of them. We worked side by side, preparing a new batch while the oven coaxed golden brown from the edges of early pies. My "toy's" stock soared about 24 percent.

The four-track recorder will always be a "toy," though. Sandra plays no musical instrument and is a reluctant singer. "When I play the radio, I get static," she says, another of her stock phrases. Hmmm, wonder if she would learn to play the autoharp?

✤

Practical lesson in 'citizenship'

For the past several years, students in Susan Glover's first-grade class at Banks Elementary School have asked me to help in one of their special assignments. One year, her class polled the school about allowing girls to wear caps inside but banning boys from doing the same. Another time, her students shared views on being called "kids."

This year, Ms. Glover helped her students learn a lesson in compassion. After completing a unit of study on "Citizenship," in which some of the lessons centered on caring for others, they decided to put learning into practice. So the class drew pictures and wrote notes to cheer up a special person. Now, Ms. Glover, her students, and I know who this person is, but the lady involved does not want to make her illness public, so she shared the notes and pictures with me, but asked that I not identify her in this column. Still, she wants Ms. Glover and her students to know how deeply their thoughtfulness touched her heart.

Several of the students drew pictures of rainbows, and rainbows have always made this lady happy. Their colors and brightness remind us of a giant smile turned upside down. Others included hearts in their drawings to express caring and love. A couple drew an angel, and having an angel on your side during a time of sickness is always a good thing. Some drew brightly colored houses to remind us of the joys of home.

One drew a long, winding road and adorned the path with friendly animals. In the center of the picture is a heart with an arrow through it. The word "Love" is enclosed inside the heart. On the bottom of some of the pictures was a series of X's and O's, universal symbols for hugs and kisses. When we are feeling bad, hugs and kisses always make us feel better. Many pictures included trees or clouds. As I looked through these drawings with their bright colors, I marveled at how these first-graders already know the things that bring us the truest joy and comfort.

This special lady and I would like to thank each of you for your kindness. We want you to know that your time and effort cheered her up. She is going to keep your drawings and get-well wishes for her recovery. Whenever she feels a little down, she will take them out, look at your drawings and read again your notes to remind her of just how many people care for her.

Thank you, Ms. Glover, for helping her students put their classroom learning into action. Students often wonder why they have to learn so many of the things we teach them in school, but I doubt that any of Ms. Glover's students will forget this lesson about "citizenship" and compassion.

Ms. Glover and her students are just one example of the good things happening in classrooms across this county—teachers who touch their students on the most basic and human level. In our state's never ending quest for higher test scores, I am glad that some teachers still remember that lessons in humanity are important, even though end of grade testing never checks for progress in that area.

I believe in this adage for teachers: "You teach some by what you say, more by what you do—but most by what you are." Ms. Glover's students are living proof of what she teaches—and what she is.

❧

A Mother's Day wish

"If you could have anything in the world for Mother's Day, what would it be?" I asked my wife, Sandra.

"World peace," she said, being a little silly. "Or…ummm… my house finally straightened up," she added.

"I'll call the UN," I replied, immediately assessing which task would be easier to accomplish.

"Anything I want. Well, I think I'd like to have all my children near me," she said seriously.

One of the real heartaches of parenthood is having your children leave the area where you live. I wanted my adult children to leave the nest and fly the coop, but not flee the territory. I wanted them out of the house and on their own—but still close enough to visit.

My daughter Sara and her husband, Mark, left North Carolina and went to Ohio for three years. They have had two children up there, so not only was my daughter 10 to 12 hours away, but so were my grandchildren. Sandra and I hoped against hope that Sara, Mark and family would come back to the Tar Heel State. They returned in August 1999.

Before Mark and Sara could return to the land of tall pines, my daughter Rachel and her husband, Toby, headed for Texas. The trip to Texas made the Ohio trek seem a stroll across the back yard. In the course of these changes, daughter Lydia headed to the Raleigh area. Just a few months later, Michael settled himself at East Carolina. Sandra and I were alone.

Can you imagine how quiet the house is? At one point in our lives Sandra and I had four kids fussing, fighting, running, and yelling. Lydia had radar that alerted her of when I went into the bathroom. As soon as I would get settled, I'd hear a frantic rap, rap, tap, tap on the door.

"Daddy, I've got to go sooooo bad!" she would plead.

Believe it or not, just the other day she was passing through town from Raleigh, experienced a call of nature, and decided to use our house for a pit stop.

Rap, rap, tap, tap.

"Daddy, I've got to go soooo bad."

How could she have known?

Where once our house crawled with kids, now our offspring shoot touch-and-gos on the runaway of our life. Where once high-pitched sibling voices railed against injustice and about whose turn it was to play Tetris, now TV announcers drone on about Elian or Jon Benet or Monica's new line of clothing or whatever worn-out subject they are using to perform the electronic lobotomy on us all.

Mother's Day is a celebration marked by dining out, sending cards, giving flowers, buying gifts. But what we'd most like to have for Mother's Day is the presence of our children, a presence that does not measure its stops in minutes. I once heard parishioners who sat in the church and constantly looked at their watches called "clock-eyed Christians." I don't want "clock-eyed kids." I am grateful that I don't have any.

Sandra and the kids were on and off beachcombers, were picnickers and putt-putt players. They sometimes visited the perfume section of J.C. Penney's and sniffed perfume samples.

Sara, Rachel, Lydia, Michael and I would sing songs from *Camelot* or *Fiddler on the Roof*. Or I'd take my guitar out and we sing "Little Playmate" or "There's a Hole in the Bucket" or "Bingo." Now, all my little playmates aren't so little...and they don't come by to play much anymore.

And I...I sometimes feel like Tevye in *Fiddler on the Roof*. Frankly, most of the time I feel like Tevye. I've l'chaym-ed and mazeltov-ed with the best of them. But "Sunrise, Sunset" still floods my eyes and leaves wet streaks down my cheeks. "Is this the little girl I carried? Is this the little boy at play? I don't remember growing older. When did they?"

Lydia reduced me to a blubbering idiot once in a restaurant by playing "Butterfly Kisses" on the jukebox. Rachel did the same thing at her wedding with the same song.

If you could have anything in the world for Mother's Day, what would it be?

"I'd like to have all my children near me."

I would, too.

Top ten marriage tips

On Thursday, Sandra and I celebrated our 27th wedding anniversary. Nearly each time I shared this tidbit of personal information, some asks: "How have you two managed to stay married so long?"

Those of you who know my satiric side will understand my standard response:

"I couldn't afford child support for four kids—and she couldn't handle half my debts."

Actually, I have realized that most people have more concern and spend more time maintaining their cars and homes than they do maintaining their marriages. We seem to suffer from the collective mythology that teaches when two people say, "I do," those magic words alone seal their relationship forever. Nothing could be further from the truth. Marriage takes care and effort.

So, in the spirit of true gratitude for a happy marriage, I offer my top ten ways for staying married.

No. 10—Always respect one another. Why does the average husband or wife get more respect on the job than at home? So many married folks feel that when they enter their home, their I.Q. drops at least 40 points. Mutual respect is fundamental.

I don't think I'll ever forget the time we were eating with a couple I knew, and the husband began chiding his wife for something she had cooked that hadn't turned out quite right. He apologized to Sandra and me for his wife's incompetence. Of course, the wife could have crawled beneath an ant's tummy by this time. All I could think was, how could this man be so insensitive and stupid. Learn this basic lesson of life: If you want respect, give respect.

No. 9—Leave the past in the past. No couple can stay married more than a quarter of a century without doing things that rile, irritate, infuriate, and annoy the other person. I know couples who, during the course of an argument, dredge up every insult, shortcoming and failure. What possible good does that do? Can you nurture a relationship with that type of ill will? The bitterness that bares its fangs poisons a relationship. Enough strikes of that venom, and the relationship dies.

No. 8—Be quick to apologize; be quick to forgive. Paul Simon wrote, "When something goes wrong, I'm the first to admit it. / The first to admit it; / But the last one to know." Not every act of insensitivity I commit is laced with malice. Sometimes, my transgressions are embroidered with stupidity. So are yours. The Bible says, "Be angry and sin not; let not the sun go down upon your wrath." When you do wrong, admit your error and apologize. When you are on the receiving end of an apology, accept it and forgive.

No. 7—Keep short accounts. Admittedly, this tip is closely connected to No. 8. If Sandra and I can admit our failings to each other and receive forgiveness, then we can make sure that we do not build walls to separate us.

Think of an offense—whether an insensitive word or deed, or an error of omission—as a brick. When we commit the transgression, we lay a brick between us on the floor. If we deal with that brick each day and move it away, then we keep the space between us open. But if we ignore that brick, then tomorrow we will place another brick or two or half dozen between us. By the time a month passes, then we have built a small wall. Six months later, we must speak to each other over the wall—sort of like Wilson and Tim Taylor.

The key is to take that first brick away every day.

No. 6—Look for the good and positive in each other. Our brains are wired to focus on the negative. Being able to spot danger is a key to our survival. When I drive down the highway, I may not notice the freshly cut grass, the tastefully placed picnic table, or the smooth pavement that allows my car to glide along. What I notice is the car pulled to the side of the road, the glass fragments from the latest traffic accident, or the potholes. Why? My health and the well being of my car depend on these observations.

Finding reasons to criticize and condemn is easy. Someone is always doing something I don't like. But people also do things I like—things that are beneficial. To give praise, I must learn to look for the positive, to search for the good.

Nowhere is this practice more important than in marriage. Kindness and appreciation help us deal with the potholes in the highway of life. Home should be a haven, not a war zone.

Well, I only made it through five tips. Maybe I'll share the other five next week. Until then, work on these five. You'll be surprised how much they will do for your relationship.

Top five marriage tips

Last week, I shared five of what I believe are the top ten tips for staying married. Today I'll complete the task. A marriage is a living creation. As such, married people must nurture each other and nurture their marriage. Too many view marriage as a ceremony or a ritual. A wedding is a ceremony with ritual overtones. However, after the wedding bells fall silent, all the rice or birdseed is swept away, the tuxedos returned and the wedding gown stored, marriage begins. In short, the work begins.

No. 5—Give each other space. Some folks have the idea that all they need do to have a strong marriage is spend time together constantly. Sandra and I have some interests we share, and each of us has interests we do not share. We spend time together on interests we share, yet we grant each other the freedom to enjoy the things we do not have in common. I don't like to be smothered, and neither does she. We need room to breathe and grow as individuals. After all, we are not clones of each other.

No. 4—Trust each other. Trust begins and ends with truthfulness. Wedged between the beginning and the end is confidence in the honor and integrity of the other person. I live by the precept that one-half truth equals one whole lie. When I give my word to anyone, I do my best to keep it.

This principle is paramount in marriage. I have known couples that hid things from each other. I've never liked deceit. When Sandra tells me something, I take her word as gospel. I believe she feels the same about me. Because we are truthful with each other, we don't end up inventing lie upon lie to cover earlier lies.

No. 3—The little things count most. A kind word. A smile. A back rub. A foot massage. A flower for no special reason. All these things are important because little things say "I love you" loudest. Little things imply attention to detail. I have never known a man or woman who got the little things right who did not also take care of the major things.

No. 2—Romance is the 10-10-10 of marriage. For city folk who may not understand 10-10-10, those three numbers refer to fertilizer. Dad once told me it meant 10 parts horse, 10 parts cow, and 10 parts hog. I think he was kidding, but I've never been sure. At any rate, a timely and healthy dose of fertilizer is a way to spark growth in plants.

Let's face it: Our lives are just too full—jobs to work, bills to pay, kids to tend and wash and feed and change. We have music lessons, little league, scouts and so on—world without end. Couples get so caught up in doing these things that they never take time for themselves.

Romance is the fertilizer of marriage. What did we do to first attract each other? Special dates? Looking our best? Holding hands and talking? Looking at the moon and stars in the bliss of solitude? Sharing hope and dreams?

Before long, two people grow so close that they experience the "sweet sorrow" of separation. What ends we pursue to woo. Once we marry, we act like a trap has closed. SLAM. Romance is over. But enduring marriages exist between people who can keep romance alive—whose hearts beat a little faster in anticipation of being together and whose eyes mist a little at the prospect of separation. A living love shines through their romance.

No. 1—Put each other first. I have only one qualification to that tip: Put God first in your lives. But after the Lord, each other must be next. The pressures of daily life can get us so caught up in doing and going that our spouse wonders if he or she even counts anymore. Men are notorious for working so much that their wives wonder if they love their jobs more than their wives. The reverse is also true.

"What about the children?" you might ask. The best gift parents can give their children is a living, vibrant, loving marriage. Children feel secure in the homes of loving parents devoted to each other. Children learn how to love, how to relate to others, and how to live for others by watching a healthy marriage.

We are far too willing to enter marriage with a wash-and-wear wedding gown and a packed parachute. We need to enter with commitment to each other and to the life we have together.

Marriage takes work and energy. Marriage requires kindness and compassion. Marriage requires self-sacrifice. All I can tell you is that from where I sit, the past 27 years have been worth the investment Sandra and I have made.

Bonds, rings, enduring things

Thirty years ago today, Sandra and I exchanged "I do's" and "I will's" during a solemn ceremony. I doubt either of us fully understood the import of all the promises we made. My ears weren't working well. My eyes had overruled my ears as I looked at the petite woman dressed in all white standing by my side.

"In sickness and in health," the Rev. Charles Webb intoned. "In poverty as in wealth. In the good that shall lighten your way and in the evil that shall darken your days. To have and to hold from this day forward as long as you both shall live."

Most couples have no idea about the source of those words. They do not come, as many suppose, from the Bible. Instead, they have passed to us in a number of variations from Anglo-Saxon times. The Anglo-Saxons were nothing if not practical, so the fact they professed their wedding vows with such concrete promises should not surprise us.

When the final "Amen" echoed through the church, and Sandra and I saluted each other with our first marital kiss, we turned to leave the church. How could we have imagined that 30 years later we would still be walking hand-in-hand?

Thirty years? What first springs to mind when I think of 30 years is retirement. In most businesses, after 30 years' service, the worker qualifies for retirement and can draw a pension. But the reward for the service Sandra and I have rendered to each other for 30 years is more costly—we pay in pearls beyond great price. Pearls of love, pearls of wisdom, pearls of devotion, pearls of romance. Too many married people know love without romance. How sad.

Thirty years? Why, that's enough time to pay off a traditional fixed-term mortgage. And, like a mortgage, we have made our payments to our marriage. We paid attention. We paid time, energy and effort. We paid in childrearing.

But my attitude towards what I have paid in marriage is not like the grudging way I pay my taxes. I pay taxes complete with weeping and wailing and grinding of teeth. Marital debts I pay with a sense of pride and satisfaction, knowing that the petite woman who stood by me that day—and has stood by me since—repays my life's time and energy with multiple returns on investment.

Marriage is like homeownership. Most homeowners take pride in their homes. I have never looked at my home as just a "house." I realize that I live in a house, but years of experiences have made that structure of sticks and bricks more than the just small building we live inside. Each nook stores a memory. Around each turn awaits a flash of family history—and usually a killer dust-bunny.

My marriage is familiar, like my home. A touch, a song, an aroma—all these and more trigger recollections that keep 30 years of marriage boiling in a timeless melting pot of the ever-present now. "Something in the way she looks," Beatle George Harrison once sang. Something, too, in the way she calls my name, sighs, combs her hair, tosses her head, raises her finger, smiles or frowns. Whether last month, last year or last decade—each experience's impression bubbles with the rest, trapped in the endless now.

Unlike a home, we can never fully pay the mortgage on marriage. That mortgage lasts as long as we both shall live.

One of my friends remarked that Sandra and I could make it to 50—not 50 the age (I've already made that figure and more) but to the magical Golden Anniversary. I had never thought about that point. We have 30 down—only 20 left to go. Why, we could perhaps make 60 or even 75.

If God is willing, though, our Golden Anniversary seems like a safe bet.

I sure hope He is.

CHAPTER TWO

DAZED, CONFUSED, AND CONFOUNDED

Midlife attacks with vengeance

I had my first major attack of mid-life crisis at 9:30 Saturday morning. Sara, my oldest daughter, and her husband John pulled away from my house with a U-Haul trailer headed for John's home in Illinois.

My little girl. Gone. Headed to the frozen North a thousand miles or more from her Mama and Daddy.

What if she needs us?

What if she needs me?

I was a trooper. Sara rarely looked me in the eye, and I returned the favor. I took a few pictures, exchanged some pleasantries, and gave my daughter the last hug I'll be able to give her for God knows how long.

Please spare me the meaningless "birds from the nest" truism. It may be true, but that truth does nothing to ease the ache I feel or fill the new emptiness in my life.

Where has time gone?

I can still see the nurse leaving the delivery room with Sara wrapped in a blanket. Only 16 months later, Rachel rested in what I called the "baby bun warmer" as she pushed a tiny, ruddy fist toward her mouth.

Lydia arrived at Lenoir Memorial just 51 minutes after

Sandra and I broke the emergency room doors. Lydia was almost exactly two years younger than Rachel.

As I approached 26, I was Daddy to three little girls.

Now Sara has finished school, is married and is gone. Rachel is in school in Greenville, a junior majoring in English at East Carolina. Lydia graduated from high school this June. My three little girls aren't little girls anymore. Two have left the nest, and we have to keep salt on Lydia's tail to keep her from flying the coup.

Even Michael is growing up so fast. He is taller than his mother and can converse on nearly any subject from the relative merits of today's super heroes to the legends of ancient Greece and Rome. He told me the other day that he wanted to be a lawyer when he grows up, but I told him he had to get an honest job.

Where have all my babies gone? Where has the past 20 years gone?

I don't remember growing older. I may have lost a half step on the base path, but I still swing a mean bat. I still have so many things I need to tell my children—so many warnings they need to hear and heed.

I told my dad that I had gone from commander to adviser with Sara and Rachel. They are both over 18, adults before the law. Before long, Lydia will be in the same league. But I don't really want control over them. I just want them to be safe and prudent and happy.

I remember all the times that Mom and Dad tried to warn and exhort me. I listened with respect, for they are my parents. But what did they know? Almost everything, I found out. The soundest financial advice I have ever received came from my father. My mother keeps telling me to slow down—that I work too much and need to cut back. I am just now beginning to realize how right she is.

I wonder if my children will look to Sandra and me as a fountain of wisdom the way I look to my parents.

Will I be ready?

I feel like such a child sometimes.

One day I realized that while Mom and Dad were not always right, they never gave me advice that they did not believe to be right. And—even more important—they always had my best interests at heart in whatever they had to say.

Michael is my connection to what I was, but Sara, Rachel and Lydia are pointing me to what I must become. I feel comfortable with the role I had when they were young like Michael. I'm not so sure I like this new role. I feel uncertain. I am facing the unknown, peering more deeply into its emptiness than I have ever had to look before.

But like it or not, this new role is mine.

Perhaps these realizations form the essence of mid-life crisis.

Awkward age an annoying presence

I am at that awkward age.

The age when my eyebrows want to stick up every which way. The age when I stay in a quandary over whether my hair can hold on long enough to turn gray before it finishes turning loose. The age where I wonder why I can find new and rechargeable batteries for any electronic device I own...but I can't find new rechargeables for me.

At 35, I had nearly unlimited stamina. I could go strong on just three or four hours sleep. I often went days on a nap now and again. Somewhere around 45, stamina deserted me. I get tired now. I don't mean sleepy—although I do get sleepy, too. And I am not talking about the good kind of tired that settles in after a hard day of profitable labor or after playing half a dozen back-to-back pick-up basketball games.

I am talking about the type of tired that makes me nod off right in the middle of stimulating conversation or events. I can be annoying—even boring. Here we are involved in animated conversation. The next thing you'll know—I've dozed off. All I need to find the path to sleepy land is a cozy chair and a comfortable temperature.

ZZZZZZZZZZ.

I have arrived at the age where annoying pains play hide and seek. A pain that touches my knee in the morning races to my lower back by breakfast. Tag. Now the winch is off to the neck or an elbow or a hand. Sometimes when I stand up, you'd think you were watching me under the blips of a strobe as the little pain Gremlin races through my joints at the speed of light.

I always figured the deterioration would be slow. Nope. I was gliding along, working hard and constantly, napping as little as possible to refresh myself, and then...The Wall. I crashed into it full speed. Didn't see it coming. No time to slow down. Just BAM.

Retirement is looking better all the time.

'Spring forward' blues

Well, they did it to us again. Sunday morning we had moved our clocks forward an hour so we could all lose even more sleep than we already lose. Instead of greeting the morning's sunlight, we can fade to gray or black.

If you haven't guessed by now, I despise the time change. I loathe Daylight Savings Time. By the decree of a power beyond my control, I lose not only an hour of sleep, but hours of sleep— one hour times the number of days in the number of months it takes me to get used to the time change.

The change wreaks havoc on my internal body clock. Even though the clock may say 6 a.m. when I rise, my body tells me it needs at least another hour of sleep. I am not interested in someone telling me I get that "hour" back at the end of October. I don't need an extra hour then. I need it now. Besides, I think the hour I get back is the shrunken ghost of the hour they stole in April.

Perhaps Daylight Savings Time was a good idea when it first started—during World War II. But I think I learned in history class somewhere that WWII is over. So why do we still "spring forward" and "fall back"? I read somewhere that "Daylight Savings Time" helped farmers grow more crops during the war. Now, the person who wrote that tidbit probably doesn't know any real farmers. All the farmers I know never consult a watch or clock to know when the time has come to begin work. They are up before dawn, on the job at dawn, and work until dark. "Daylight Savings Time" certainly has—and had—no impact on farmers at all.

As things stand now, we have seven months of Daylight Savings Time and five months of standard time. Add to this confusion the fact that two states don't do the "Daylight Savings Time" thing at all. Indiana and Arizona refuse to play the time shift game. Those states stay on standard time year round. What if you live in Ohio and want to call someone in Indiana. You'd have to remember that the next state over is an hour behind you—for seven months.

I am not sure I object to "Daylight Savings Time" per se. I think what I really hate is changing time twice a year—and upsetting my body's clock in the process. Why can't we pick a time and stick with it. If most folks like "Daylight Savings Time" during the part of the year that we have sunny, warm weather—more power to them. Let's just stay on DST. After all, we are on that time most of the year anyway.

I want to share the best suggestion I've heard and read about this time claptrap. Mountain and Eastern zones would stay on Standard Time year-round. They would never go back to Daylight Savings Time. Western and Central time zones would stay on Daylight Savings Time year-round. They would never go back to the current "Standard Time."

This plan would immediately reduce the number of time zones in the United States from four to two. About half the nation would be in one time zone: Eastern. The other half would be on Western time. California would no longer be three hours behind us—just two. Los Angeles and Seattle would have the same time as Boise and Boulder. Chicago and Little Rock would be on the same time as New York and Atlanta.

The best part of this plan is that regardless of where you live, you would never have to "spring forward" again. Your body clock could go on ticking without taking a licking from losing an hour of sleep.

I may be the only person in Kinston, Lenoir County, North Carolina, or the United States who cares about this subject. However, judging by the foggy looks that greet me after we all "spring forward," I think others care once their minds clear. Consider this fact: Time zone zombies work in our factories, fix our food, doctor and nurse our sick, teach our kids, and drive on our highways. We must end this tawdry time manipulation before some time-shift zombie runs you off the road or builds your next car.

Write to Congress! Write to the Legislature! Write to the Governor! Tell them all that we demand one time...forever. End the springing forward. End the falling back. Can I get an Amen?

❧

Wintertime blues

The 1950's rocker Eddie Cochrane was best known for his song "Summertime Blues." Over the sound of his driving guitar, he moaned, "There ain't no cure for the summertime blues." I supposed that in some parts of the country, summer causes the blues. The oppressive heat and muggy humidity are enough to cause some sort of blue funk, I guess. I usually cure summertime blues with air conditioning.

The wintertime blues afflict me far worse than anything that hits in the summer. Frankly, winter combines all the elements that grind down my body and soul—cold, dark, gloom, dead grass, bare trees, short days. Now, I am sure some of you just love the winter. If so, your definition of fun probably includes riding in an open ski lift to the top of a mountain to risk your life shooting down a snowy slope while you dodge trees and less accomplished skiers.

One of the most miserable academic quarters I spent at The Ohio State University was the winter I took "Ice Skating" as a physical education elective. I had taken soccer in the fall.

Winter quarter I decided to take a class in something I knew nothing about. Ice skating was perfect. The closest I had ever come to skating on the ice was when my feet slipped from under me and I busted my...well, you know. Learning. Education. Challenge. Ice skating.

Did I ever make a wrong decision. What I learned about ice skating had nothing to do with figure eights, fancy spins, and jumps. Did you know that trying to find the perfect tightness for laces is essential? If I laced my skates too tightly, then the pressure arrested the circulation to my feet and they went to sleep. As a result, I couldn't stand on them. If I tied the skates too loosely, then they did not support my ankles. I spent the entire quarter searching for the perfect tension. Never did find it.

Ice skating was a three-hour class. For some reason, I never stopped to think that ice skating meant being on this huge, thick sheet of ice for most of that time. Each week, I entered the rink, clung to the wall, and tried to stay in something close to an upright position. I looked like a 230-pound baby taking my first, fledgling steps, but without the grace or diaper a baby has. Zip—my feet flew out from under me. Bang—I hit the ice. The pattern became climb back up, cling to the wall, collect myself—and try again. Zip. Bang. Climb. Cling. Try again.

As I worked on zipping-banging, climbing-clinging, two parts of my body became increasingly cold—and my two feet were only one part I'm talking about. I'm probably the only student in the history of Ohio State who was ever treated for frostbite of the—to quote Forrest Gump—buttocks. Why did I write about this? I'll probably need some more sessions with my therapist now.

But that ice skating experience symbolizes so much of what winter is. I hate being cold. I hate having to wake up in the dark and come home from work in the dark. Winter's cold makes the day shrink up. Only the warmth of spring can entice the daylight to stay a little longer.

I love Down East in the spring because I adore green sprouting everywhere. I love Down East in the summer because that spring green ripens into a full lushness. I love Down East in the fall because the green mixes with other colors, creating a delightful display. I love the Bahamas in the winter.

Winter means cold and chill. That 45-degree temperature would be bearable if the wind didn't drive it into my flesh like so many dull nails. Winter assaults my weakest points—my hands, my feet, the nape of my neck.

If I could spend winter in the perfect way, I'd eat a big tasty meal and then find some blankets and a bed. Come wake me when spring gets here. Until then....

Stymied by soccer

For some reason my son, Michael, decided to go out for sports in this his senior year. Michael is musical, artistic, and academically gifted, but somehow I never thought of him as a high school athlete. Naturally, when he looked around for a sport, he did not choose basketball or baseball—sports that I understand. Instead, he decided to try out for the soccer team.

"But why soccer, son?" I asked in a plaintiff voice.

"Because, Dad," he said, looking at me as if I just stepped from a chunk of the Ice Age, "soccer is the world's most popular sport. Every country has a team. And I also get to legally slam into people."

So in the scorching heat of summer, he headed to soccer practice where he ran, and kicked a soccer ball, and ran, and passed a soccer ball, and ran. By the first game, Michael had dropped about 12 pounds. Now when he runs laps, he hardly even pants—he used to huff and puff like a room filled with bagpipe players.

Being a supportive father, I headed to the first game. Little did I realize that I only thought I knew nothing about this game. My lack of soccer understanding was similar to a black hole. For instance, I saw players jumping out of bounds to throw the ball in. Sometimes one of our players would streak to the goal only to be whistled for "off sides."

"Off sides!" I stood and shouted in a rage at the dimwitted

official. "How could he be off sides when they didn't even snap the ball!" I felt at tug at my belt. Sandra was pulling me back to my seat. Another soccer parent leaned over to explain "off sides" in soccer. As I understand it, an offensive player may not advance toward the goal unless a defensive player other than the goalie is closer to the goal than the offensive player is—and the moon must not be hanging low in the western sky and Mercury must be aligned with Mars in the Seventh House—or something like that. Although I am not sure exactly what off sides may be, I do understand one thing—soccer has no equivalent to the "fast break" in basketball. No wonder the scores are so low.

I saw a player intentionally kick the ball out of bounds. I looked for a flag—that had to be something akin to "intentional grounding" in football. I turned to my knowledgeable friend.

"Why didn't pinkie [the ref] give that guy a flag or yellow card or green card or something?"

"Oh, that's legal in soccer," my friend said. "You see, when the offense is moving the ball and the defense is out of position, the defenders kick the ball out of bounds to give their side a chance to set up for the play."

Although I enjoy watching the Hawks play, I still don't have a handle on a "corner kick," a "penalty kick," and a "free kick." I don't know what they are, when they happen, and what distinguishes one from another. Michael has tried to help, but he usually ends up throwing his hands up and stomping away, wondering why someone who can understand the subtleties of Shakespeare can't grasp these simple soccer concepts.

When I first started watching the games (or matches or whatever they are called), everything on the field looked like chaos. Frankly, I found the game a little boring because the contest offered almost no scoring, no sacks, no field goals, no punt returns, no home runs, no slam dunks—nothing I could get hold of. But as I have watched more of these contests, things seem to be sorting out a bit. Now I can holler "off sides," "handball," and "yellow card" with the best of them. Of course,

I usually holler these terms at the wrong times.

However, I have discovered that—according to the soccer fans in the stands—officials in soccer are just as blind and mentally challenged as officials everywhere.

Now, that's something I can understand, Pinkie.

Rafting 'The River of Noon Day Sun'

My wife, Sandra, and I sat at the kitchen table of the cottage at 200 Croakin' Frog Lane in Otto, NC. I couldn't believe my ears. My brother, John, and his wife, Gisele, had just suggested that we go whitewater rafting.

Now, the mention of whitewater rafting probably sets some of your adrenal glands running amuck, but anything to do with rafting, white water, and rivers creates an entirely different bodily reaction in me. You see, rafting means motion, and motion can mean motion sickness. I've gotten sick watching my rubber ducky bobbing in the bathtub.

But Sandra was excited about the trip, and so were John and Gisele's kids, Dan, Jess, and John Henry. So, what could I do? Showing the white feather was not an option. I could only hope that the Rolling Thunder Whitewater Rafting Company would not have a life vest able to circumnavigate my girth.

Monday morning we left for Almond, NC. I am not really sure if we passed through Almond or not. I do know that roughly 10 minutes west of Bryson City, we turned onto the premises of Rolling Thunder River Company. We walked to the desk, and Vicky, who manned the desk, shoved a piece of paper toward me.

"You and everybody in your party will need to sign this waiver," Vicky said. I read the waiver. It said—in short—that we were risking death, injury, fractures, abrasions, cuts, and everything just shy of death by chocolate (which would have been okay with me), and that we would hold the company guiltless if we suffered any of these mishaps on our way down the Nantahala River. We also promised to hold the company blameless even if our injury or death directly resulted from their negligence.

Do what?

Frankly, as I read those words, I hoped anew the life vest (they called it a personal flotation device—a PFD) wouldn't fit. But then, how could I send my poor wife, not to mention my niece and nephews, on a trip I was unwilling to risk myself? I comforted myself by thinking that the Rolling Thunder waiver sounded pretty much like the one a person signs prior to surgery—except for the negligence part.

After being outfitted with a PFD and paddle and after listening to a safety talk, we boarded the bus that would take us to the point of no return.

"How many of you have never done this before?" the bus driver asked. My hand was one of about two dozen that streaked upward.

"Well, just keep your hands and head inside the windows, stay seated, and leave the driving to me," he said with a well-timed delivery that told me we hand-raisers had just become the victims of his first joke. How could he joke about this trip when I had just signed away my rights to sue?

The driver also explained that the Nantahala River is always cold. The temperature of its water stays between 45 and 48 degrees. A huge pipe at the bottom of the Nantahala Reservoir provides water for the river. That water has never felt the warming rays of the sun.

I discovered later that the water in the river rarely feels the rays of the sun because "Nantahala" means "river of the noon day sun." The Nantahala flows through a gorge so deep that the only time the river receives direct sunlight is at noon. And here I was without a wet suit.

Question: What is worse than being wet?

Answer: Being wet and cold.

We finally put in for this eight-mile experience of rapids and cold water. Where we would be rafting, the Nantahala offers a variety of rapids: Level One, Level Two, Level Two-Plus, and a Level Three. Level One means you get a few bumps and some light splashing. Level Two means you experience more furious bumps and lots of splashing. Level Two-Plus means you're going to get enough splashed water in your raft to sit for the next few miles ankle deep in 45-degree water.

Imagine having to navigate through the Whirlpool, the Needle, and the Bump. Imagine passing huge boulders with these names: Pyramid Rock, Picnic Rock, Jaws. Thankfully, we had a guide in our raft. His name was Anson. Anson was humorous, knowledgeable and compassionate.

Safety was Anson's prime concern so he could also become serious, even severe. For example, we came upon one raft stuck on a rock and a passenger was preparing to climb out. Anson blew a long blast on his whistle and yelled, "Stay in the raft! Do not leave your raft!" Then he helped free the raft so the group could continue their trek.

As we moved down the river, we gained confidence. Leigh Ann, an 11-year-old New Jersey girl who occupied the seat right in front of me, wore a deer caught in headlights expression when we first started down the river. About halfway through the trip, she had the air of an old salt.

We headed directly for rocks only to swirl around them. We did 360's with our raft and even threaded the Needle—backwards. A couple of miles into the trek, I realized something: I was having fun. We all were.

And the longer we traveled down the Nantahala, the more of a team we became. At first, when Anson would yell, "Paddle Forward!" we looked more like a spider with a neurological disorder than a rafting crew. But as we worked together and overcame our fear, we moved like a finely built Swiss watch.

I left the river realizing just how professional and thorough the folks at Rolling Thunder were. I left feeling like I had been a small part of a synchronized rafting ballet.

Mining for mountains gems

I have often wondered why most of the biographies

of British writers included a description of "a trip to the continent"—as they called their mainland European excursions. That trip was always part of their education. The Brits had formal schooling, but travel was the living complement to formal instruction. A recent trip to western North Carolina gave me insight into the value of travel as education.

Sandra and I visited with my brother John, his wife Gisele, and their children John Henry, Jessica and Dan. John and Gisele had rented a two-bedroom, bath and a half "cottage" complete with a loft and a breath-taking view of the Smoky Mountains.

On Saturday evening, Gisele read through several brochures detailing possible excursions during our stay in Otto, NC. Whitewater rafting. Horseback riding. Gem mining. Now, gem mining struck a nerve with me. White water rafting and horseback riding share one thing in common—erratic motion on a barely controllable, powerful medium. At the time Gisele was reading the brochures, I was actively listening for some alternative to a river filled with rapids or a horse.

"Gem mining sounds good," I said, hoping my tone indicated real interest. We all discussed the idea. The young folks were excited about it—and so was Sandra, always young at heart. So we agreed. On Sunday we would head to a gem mining establishment. A deep sense of victory washed over me. I had avoided the horse and the raft.

But I had no idea just how fascinating the gem mining would be. We ended up at Gold City Gem Mine located off Highway 441 in Franklin, NC. I think John and Gisele had the idea that we'd get a couple of bags of dirt, sluice them in the flume and be done with the whole deal. But I asked a few questions. Buckets of dirt are not all created equal, I found out. Some have more dirt than stones. They are the cheap buckets. As with most things in life, you get what you pay for. So we decided to spring for a more expensive bucket. That decision turned out to be wonderful.

Do you have any idea what it is like to sit at a flume with water coursing by, sink a box with wire on the bottom into that water—and find gemstones? At first, the young people and I would place all of our finds in front of us, and a Gold City employee would come by periodically, knock off the rocks—and leave the gemstones. His or her patter went something like this:

"Rock. Rock. Ruby. Rock. Rock. Garnet. Sapphire. Rock. Ruby. Rock."

Sandra was not sluicing. Sluicing involves getting mud on fingers and under fingernails. Neither prospect appeals to her. So, she used a cup to dip dirt into the boxes so the rest of us could find the stones. Evidently, John and Gisele shared her aversion to the sluice. However, as John and Gisele's kids began finding beautiful stones—emeralds, topaz, amethyst—the next thing I knew, John had found a spot by the flume.

"Dirt me," he said to Sandra. Now, I have not figured out if he just got excited about the stones—or if he looked at the five-gallon bucket of dirt, rocks and stones and decided if he wanted to leave Gold City within the next few hours, he'd better help sluice.

The thing that most amazed me was that when we started the process, not one of us could tell a rock from a ruby or a sapphire or garnet. But as the Gold City employees took a little time to explain what to look for, they were kicking off less rocks and saying, "Ruby. Garnet. Sapphire" more and more.

I was so excited about gemstones that when I returned to Kinston, I visited the public library and checked out a couple of books so I could read up on gems. Right now I've got a half-pound of silver and blue topaz stones in a rock tumbler. I think I'll do the emeralds next. Know anyone who can cut and polish rubies, sapphires and garnets?

By the way, what is the difference between a ruby and a sapphire? Answer: Both rubies and sapphires, which occur naturally in the mountains of North Carolina, are gem-quality corundum. Ruby is red because it contains iron traces. Any corundum that is not a ruby is a sapphire.

Enhanced education. Gotta love it.

Pollen begets misery

I didn't really need the newspaper to tell me. My reddened eyes and occasional bouts with chain sneezing proved to me that the warm temperatures raising our spirits loosed a blunderbuss of pollen. Still, the headline "Pollen bomb explodes in state" affirmed what my body was saying—pollen, pollen, everywhere.

Just how serious is the problem right now?

According to information posted on the National Allergy Bureau's website, on April 10, every cubic meter of outside air in the Charlotte area contained 2,058 pollen particles. A cubic meter is a little bigger that a cubic yard. To help put that number in perspective, on March 30, the number of pollen particles floating in a cubic meter was SIX. For most of the year, the pollen count in North Carolina hovers in the 60s to 70s. Those numbers must be higher for Eastern North Carolina since we have more plants and fewer buildings and parking lots than Charlotte.

When spring first arrives, the fancy of young plants turns to thoughts of long-distance romance—and the pollen bomb explodes. We poor humans just happen to get in the way, the victims of nature's promiscuous pollinating.

Have you ever seen different types of pollen through a microscope? Ragweed is a common cause of springtime discomfort. A pollen particle from ragweed—blown up several thousand of thousand times—looks something like a soccer ball produced by the Marquis de Sade. Sharp prickles cover the soccer-ball surface, complete with little pins to irritate the tender flesh of your eyes and sinus passages. Oak pollen is a cross between a sphere and a triangle, an odd shape guaranteed to aggravate. Grasses have pollens. Trees have pollens. Flowers have pollens.

Could someone please pass me a tissue and the eye drops?

As I surveyed the allergy bureau's website, product of

the American Academy of Allergy, Asthma and Immunology, I learned some fascinating things about allergies. For instance, nearly 36 million people in the United States suffer from hay fever (medical name, allergic rhinitis). Hay fever may sound innocent enough, but this springtime malaise is expensive. In 1993, combined costs of treating allergic rhinitis totaled $3.4 billion—$2.3 billion for medications and another $1.1 billion for doctor visits. In addition to medical costs, allergies cost this nation in lost productivity. In 1998, the estimate cost of absenteeism and reduced productivity was $250 million.

Sinusitis is a sinus inflammation, and 31 million of us develop sinusitis in any given year. Sinus inflammations result in an average of four missed days of work per year per person. Do the math. Those figures mean people suffering from sinusitis miss more than 120 million days of work annually.

How many boxes of tissues or rolls of toilet paper do those figures represent? Springtime pollens must cost trees their lives by the acre. However, about now, with my eyes red and swollen and itching, all I can think is, "It serves you trees right."

I know. Just a couple of months ago, I complained about being cold. Now, in the midst of this toasty weather, I'm complaining again. But if an evil sandman has never dumped a truckload of grit into your eyes, then you have no idea just how pitiful I am right now.

My vision is blurry, my breathing is raspy, and I am about to seek Dr. Mark Green to help me because he always solves the most complex medical problems in an hour on "ER." Dr. Green, please just give me five minutes. And please keep Dr. Benton away. He'll want to remove my sinuses. Then again, how bad could that be?

If you suffer from spring pollen, know this: I feel your pain. Pray for a steady rain to wash this pollen right out of the air. But now I need to try to get some rest. HEPA filter, please don't fail me now.

(To visit the National Allergy Bureau website, log on to www.aaaai.org/nab/)

Wisdom of the ages

On Wednesday, August 1, I arrived at the halfway point of my life. The good news is, since I am almost 51, I am on target to live to nearly 102. By now some of you cynics are wondering how in the world I came to such a conclusion. Elementary, I assure you. Somewhere I read a proverb that says that when a person has his or her wisdom teeth removed, half that person's life is over. Since I understood the importance of that insight, I did my best to keep my wisdom teeth as long as possible. Wednesday, I finally bid them farewell.

More than a quarter century ago, I sacrificed my top two wisdom teeth through simple extraction. I was about 25. Dr. Edwards, my dentist at that time, never shared the wisdom tooth proverb with me. He seemed to have the wild idea that yanking out my scrubby wisdom teeth was a small price to pay for good dental hygiene. Obviously, top wisdom teeth don't count for proverbial reckoning. Since I had those teeth pulled at 25, had that been the halfway point of my life, today I'd be...well, you know.

Then Dr. Edwards popped the question:

"When do you want to have those bottom wisdom teeth removed? You'll have to go to the oral surgeon for that."

I was stunned.

"I'll let you know when those teeth start bothering me," I said meekly.

I am not sure Dr. Edwards understood the full impact of combining the terms "oral" and "surgeon." Loosely translated from the original Greek and Latin, "oral surgeon" means "we are going to make painful cuts inside your mouth in order to yank, pull, break and/or pulverize those nasty teeth that may or may not give you problems in the future."

So I waited. Sure enough, 25 years later the wisdom tooth on the bottom left began bothering me. I went to my current dentist, Dr. Doug Hill, who referred me to an oral surgeon in

Greenville. My plan was to sacrifice only the wisdom tooth that was causing me problems. But the oral surgeon convinced me that since he had to sedate me anyway, and since both teeth needed to come out eventually, we might as well make it a one-stop procedure. One sedation. One period of healing. One concentrated time of pain and irritation. We were listening.

Have you ever noticed how glib some folks are? Here was this fellow I barely knew talking about putting me to sleep, invading my gums, and somehow getting those wicked wisdom teeth out. Not only did I have to deal with all the oral pain and suffering, I had to pay a goodly chunk of change to him, which caused a condition known as "attrition of the hip." All the suffering on my side—all the fun on his. How could that arrangement be fair?

I have consoled myself with the thought that, eventually, my mouth will heal, that the stitches scoring the side of my mouth will go away, and that I will be able to eat solid food again—perhaps within the next several months.

But I have greater consolation than these trivialities. According to folk wisdom, a long life stretches before me. I have just as much life ahead as I have experienced so far. Another half century is mine.

One day, Willard Scott or Al Roper (or whoever is doing the weather on "The Today Show") will announce: "Mike Parker of Kinston, North Carolina, is 101 today. Mike attributes his long life to keeping his wisdom teeth as long as possible. Happy birthday to a handsome fellow."

But for right now, pass the painkiller...please.

World weighted against rotund southpaw

I read about a new group that is entering the twin battlefields of political correctness and litigation. People who exceed the upper limits of so-called "normal weight" are objecting to being the targets of slurs and contempt. Fat people, noted for their happy-go-lucky natures, are fighting back in the form of lawsuits carrying hefty price tags.

I am disappointed that organizers did not contact me before entering this fray. I have not done well at all about keeping my New Year's resolution of losing 50 of the hundred pounds I need to drop to bring me to nearly normal weight.

I can understand why fat folks are fighting back. People say the stupidest things. I don't know how many people—sometimes strangers and sometimes friends—see my rotundity and become instant experts on weight loss. Everyone seems to have a foolproof plan to help me unload my excess baggage.

"Drink a cup of grapefruit juice for breakfast, eat an apple or an orange for lunch, and crunch two rice cakes with Chinese tea for supper, and you'll be surprised at how much weight you'll lose," one unwanted adviser counseled.

Yeah, right. I've always wanted to try that new prisoner-of-war diet.

Did this idiot realize that I have to work?

When my mom used to take me clothes shopping as a boy, the clerks hustled me off to the "husky" section. Did that mean I had become a sled dog?

How about "plump"? Sounds like an afflicted leaky faucet to me.

"You're so fat that I bet your wife has to hug and chalk to get all way around you," some half-wit offered.

"Naw. She just uses her bionic extension arms," I said.

I have had the misfortune of eating out with some people who seem to eye me on the sly during the meal.

"You don't eat much for a fat guy," they say with a smile.

After that kudo, I was waiting for the ultimate compliment: "You sure don't sweat much for a fat man."

However, I must admit that I am not ready to file lawsuits over the boorish comments some make. If I were going to sue over anything, I think I would sue the whole country for making it so hard to be left-handed in a culture geared specifically for righties.

Ever fire a rifle only to have the hot shell casing shoot past your nose as smoke burned your eyes?

I have.

Ever notice that every tool in the world fits the right hand? Place that tool in the left hand and its usefulness disappears.

I am not a golfer, but I have picked up a club before. That's when I discovered if I wanted to play the game, I would have to buy a special set of left-handed clubs.

A left-handed baseball pitcher is a "southpaw." Southpaw? Did I suddenly lose my hands and become an animal? I don't believe I have ever heard of a "northpaw."

What is a "left-handed compliment"? According to one dictionary, it is a compliment with "a concealed, secondary and opposite meaning."

Is that a left-handed definition?

A screw or bolt with a "left-handed thread" tightens by turning it counterclockwise.

And how about being out in "left field"? "Away from the center of action," a dictionary says.

Yet, lefties have distinguished themselves in a number of fields. I'll make a point with just one: baseball. Ever hear of Babe Ruth? He was a southpaw. So was Lou Gehrig. Ted Williams and George Brett, too. David Justice and Fred McGriff are lefties.

I think I'll start a movement. We can meet on the Left Bank and sing Kum Bah Yah counterclockwise.

Lefties of the world, unite!

Left on!

Medical education...the painful way

Sandra and I returned home from visiting my mom on New Year's Day. I have already written about the snow and cold we endured in Ohio, so I won't rehash my complaints here. Little did I know that they day after I returned, North Carolina was going to be dumped on. Wednesday evening—snow and ice. On Thursday, at least eight more inches of snow fell atop the snow and ice already covering the ground.

Add to the discomfort of this weather—weather, I might add, that I had to get into because of job demands—a new experience. The evening of New Year's Day, as I pulled the blanket to my chin and rolled over for a good night's sleep, someone took a blow torch and tried to burn off my left big toe.

I sat up, clicked on the light, and examined my toe. The poor thing was red, swollen and running its own little fever. I would have kissed it, but I couldn't get my toe near my lips. I sent my mind on a search. Had I banged my beloved toe against something? But a quick memory check revealed no dings that would set my toe on fire.

The next day at Dobbs, I hobbled around like an overweight version of Chester from "Gunsmoke." Every time I had to move to another location, I calculated the shortest route. After all, my walking pattern that day was: step—blowtorch—step—blowtorch.

"I must have a touch of the gout," I jokingly remarked to a couple of co-workers. Before this experience, I had been familiar with gout only through a definition for the ailment supposedly given by the 19th English Baptist preacher, Charles Spurgeon. Someone once asked Spurgeon, who suffered from gout, to share the difference between arthritis and gout. Spurgeon reportedly replied: "If you put your hand in a vise and turn the handle until the pain is unbearable—that's arthritis. Give that handle five more turns—that's gout."

I called my daughter Sara, an RN, and her husband, Mark, also an RN, answered.

"Is Sara home?"

"She's giving the girls a bath," Mark said.

"Well, Mark, let me ask you about something." I describe the pain, the swelling, the redness...and the pain. Mark asked a couple of other questions.

"Mr. Parker, it sounds like you've got a case of gout."

"Gout? What is gout?"

Gout is a build up of uric acid in one or more joints, Mark said. He told me how doctors generally treated the condition. About that time, Sara came to the phone.

"Tell Sara what you told me and see what she thinks,"

Mark said and left to take over baby duties. I went through the description and answered her assessment questions.

"Daddy, sounds like gout to me." She reeled off causes, indications, contraindications, and typical modes of treatment. I knew her medical education would pay off one day. I suddenly developed a new interest in gout. Of course, I went online. I can't share much here, but I do want to share just a couple of things.

The National Institute of Arthritis and Musculoskeletal and Skin Diseases maintains a website that defines "gout" in these words: "Gout is one of the most painful rheumatic diseases. It results from deposits of needle-like crystals of uric acid in the connective tissue, joint spaces, or both."

Talk about being sorry I asked. Sara and Mark had told me about the crystals of uric acid—which is bad enough. Kidneys filter uric acid and send it to the bladder in the form of urine. That meant something akin to urine was crystallizing in my big toe. [Shudder.]

What both Sara and Mark failed to mention, probably out of kindness, was the "needle-like" structure of these crystals. Not only did I have a component of urine in my big toe, but this substance was also forming itself into needles just so it could afflict me.

Thank goodness my gout has turned off its blowtorch...for now. I'd just as soon avoid a repeat performance.

Tar Heel 'Clampett' visits Beverly Hills

Okay. The headline is a little misleading. I did go through Beverly Hills while I was visiting Los Angeles, California, but the main center of operations was the Marriott in Manhattan Beach. Still, two main thoughts crowded my head as I navigated the great concrete rivers of bumper-to-bumper traffic known as Interstate 405.

"Whee-doggy!" was the first one.

I left LAX—that's Los Angeles International Airport for

all you who do not speak airport lingo—on a 10-minute trip to Manhattan Beach. On the plane I sat near two California residents on the trip from Memphis to LAX, and both assured me that if I would just head down Sepulveda Boulevard, that I would be there in no time. "No time" turned into two hours. Our party, which thankfully included two women, decided to call the Marriott and get directions.

When I left the Hertz lot, I must have turned the wrong way and headed to Santa Barbara. Sepulveda goes a long way, I'm here to tell you. I think I had been going in some sort of circular path because once we hit the 405, we were just a few miles from Rosecrans Avenue and the Marriott.

Of course, "a few miles" has no relation to actual time on a California freeway. In North Carolina, you can roughly figure about 20 minutes or less per 15 miles. Along the 405 at "rush hour"—and I'd like to meet the idiot who coined that phrase— I drove 1.5 miles every 20 minutes. I soon learned that every hour in Los Angeles is "rush hour."

The great river of traffic never ebbs—and rarely flows.

Driving in LA is an art with Zen overtones. Here's a rule of thumb. If you need to cross three of six lanes of traffic, look at the car immediately behind you in the next lane. If that car is a Porsche, Mercedes or Jaguar, turn on the blinker and pull on over. Repeat process. No one driving one of those cars is going to hit a Mercury Grand Marquis, which is what I was driving.

Here's the reason. In California, drivers of expensive vehicles assume anyone driving an auto that costs less than theirs probably is not carrying enough liability insurance to cover the damage in case of a fender bender.

By the same token, if the car in the next lane behind you is of lesser value than yours, stay the course unless you want someone in a 1962 Volkswagen running up the tailpipe of your Grand Marquis.

On one excursion, we passed a Budget Rental Car company. The Beverly Hills Budget Rent-a-Car has a couple of dozen cars—all Mercedes, Jaguars or Porsches. Budget rental cars—Beverly Hills style. I could hear Lester Flatt and Earl

Scruggs playing in the background. All I needed was a jug to blow on.

"Whee-doggy!"

After creeping down the exit to Rosecrans Avenue, we made a right, coasted about five lights, and turned left on Nash-Parkway and into the entrance to the Marriott. Three of my party unloaded the luggage and entered the motel. I went to find a place to park. A huge parking garage stood attached to the Marriott, so I wheeled in. I took a ticket and explained to the attendant that I was a guest in the motel. She smiled.

"Oh, that's fine. They'll give you a pass at the desk so you can just have the parking fee charged to your room. That way you won't have to pay every time you go out."

"What is the fee?" I asked.

"Eleven dollars a day."

"Whee-doggy!" I replied.

And what was my second main thought?

I kept tapping my heels.

"There's no place like home...there's no place like home...."

Lessons that dancing teaches

Aging affects people in a variety of ways. For me, my memory is what I miss the most. Each year Mary Beth Dawson invites Sandra and me to attend the annual recital for Dance, ETC. Most years, at Sandra's prodding, I reluctantly go. Each year as I leave, I wonder what possible reasons I could have invented for not wanting to go in the first place.

The beauty, strength and grace that Mary Beth's students display always leave me amazed. How can these kids do these complex movements, not only in rhythm, but also with smiles on their faces? As I watched this year's show, "Dance with Me Tonight!" I again marveled.

Despite the years I spent as a newspaper reporter and editor, I must confess that beauty still touches me somewhere deep inside. Perhaps my appreciation for beauty stems from the things I had to keep up with and write about as a journalist. We live in a world that has too much horror, too much death, too much crime, too many drugs, and too much abuse.

But we live in a world that offers a full spectrum of beauty as well. A touching illustration of that beauty is watching young people dance their hearts out before an audience that roots for them to hit every step and nail every landing. Part of that beauty is seeing nearly two dozen girls, dressed in their peach costumes, use music from "Last Dance" to glide from spot to spot as they make profound exertion seem effortless.

Beauty is seeing more than a dozen young women combine their talents to transform their bodies into the bow of the Titanic as they lift one of their troupe into the air—all to the movie's evocative theme song, "My Heart Will Go On."

The beauty I saw Saturday night was not the beauty of a delicate flower. This beauty is sterner stuff. This beauty is born of strength, of discipline, and of team effort and hard work. This beauty can do a back flip, a forward roll, or a one-handed cartwheel. This beauty can dance nearly an entire number en pointe. I can barely stand on my feet sometimes. What strength must muscles develop to hold the entire weight of a dancer's body on the toes?

I saw the aura of self-confidence, the appeal of agility, the sprightliness of speed, and the beauty of balance. I saw young men and young women, girls and boys, with shoulders and backs straight—always conscious of how both the line of movement and pause from movement impact the eye.

Behind all that I saw another kind of beauty—the beauty of caring parents who sacrifice time, money and effort to give their children a chance to learn how to be an artist who can combine music and movement. Each year the Dance, ETC. dads dance a number. The moms respond with a dance of their own. Imagine the message the kids receive when they see Mom and Dad pay the price to master some of the skills of the art of dance. I saw the beauty of committed teachers who give of themselves way more than the price of a lesson can ever compensate. How can you put a price on reaching into a child's soul and helping give birth to the artist there?

Helping turn that artist loose can be a thankless task. That task requires hours of work, both in the studio and at home. That task requires discipline to count those steps again and again—spending time that child could use for watching TV or playing a video game or taking a nap. The child pays the price in tired muscles, in disappointment, in frustration. But the reward—the applause of an audience who sees and loves the work—makes the effort to excel worthwhile.

"Hard work equals excellence" is a lesson seldom taught anymore. But for any child who enters a dance studio, that lesson is one of the first ones he or she learns. That lesson is one of life's most important ones.

જે

Mother's Day blessing

Blessings sometimes come swaddled in strange wrappings. I was reminded of that fact this past Mother's Day.

Church ended, so we headed to the Golden Corral for lunch. The parking lot was surprisingly full even at 11:45. I guess some folks skipped church to take Mom out for a special day. The line slithered outside, so we took our place in the sun. Before long we were inside and getting closer to the cash register by the moment. Only two more groups stood between us and the promise of food.

"May I have your attention please," a voice announced over the intercom. Of course, we weren't listening closely, but we did catch something about a "car on fire." We looked at each other, shrugged, and stepped closer to the register.

In less than a minute, we heard the announcement more clearly.

"A blue car parked near the corner is on fire."

Michael and I looked at each other, bolted from the restaurant, and arrived just in time to see flames leaping from beneath the hood of a 1988 blue Toyota. OUR car was on fire. As we watched, someone sprayed a fire extinguisher through the grill to try to smother the flames. I opened the door and tried to pop the hood latch several times.

"The fire's probably melted the latch," a bystander said. By this time, Sandra and Lydia had joined us. We all stood looking at the burned spot on the hood where the paint had changed from a light blue to dingy brown and peeled away. Several of us again tried to open the hood. It refused to budge.

Members of the Kinston Fire Department pulled up. I was confident the fire was out, but who could know for sure. I mean, we couldn't exactly look under the hood. Two firefighters approached with an ax and pry bar in hand. They went to work on the hood. Metal bent and twisted, but the hood stayed shut. A couple of attacks from the side did nothing other than turn up an edge of the hood—and leave a deep impression on the front left fender.

"Man, Toyotas are tough," said one firefighter, sweat streaming down his face. "I've got one with over 200,000 miles."

"This one's only got 156,000," I said. "I don't guess it'll hit 200,000."

After the firefighters turned up enough of the hood to allow the business end of the fire hose to get to the engine, one guy sprayed water underneath the hood. Next, they attacked with a bolt cutter, clipped the latch, and pried open the hood.

The battery, a fuse box, and all the wiring looked like someone had decided to have French fried auto as a Mother's Day special. Two plastic containers auditioned for the next remake of "The Blob." The asphalt beneath the car appeared soft and sticky. The fire was out, but the fret just beginning. I made a couple of calls and ordered a wrecker. Cell phones are handy items.

"Might as well eat as we wait," I said.

I looked at the line of people waiting for lunch. When we first arrived, the line snaked like an Eastern rattler. Now it looked like a monster anaconda. I went inside and found a manager.

"That was our car that caught on fire," I explained. "We were just about ready to order when we heard the announcement. Please tell me I won't have to get in the back of the line."

"Just find a table and take a seat," Dalton Stocks said. "I'll have a waitress take your order."

I was so relieved. Before long, we had drinks, and the waitress had our orders. Manager Stocks brought me the bill. It showed "0.00" as the balance. I examined the bill, dumbfounded.

"Sorry for your trouble," he said. "Just wanted to do a little something for you."

I looked at the bill again, looked at him, and looked at Michael and Lydia, who sat amazed.

"Sorta restores your faith in people," Lydia said.

I nodded to her. For some reason, I couldn't speak right then.

Little things make Thanksgiving

I have finally arrived at an age where big dreams and plans no longer kindle zeal in my soul. Once I dreamed of Pulitzer prizes, fame, and fortune. I had my five-year plan intact. I was going to think and grow rich. Just so you'll know, I have started working on my second million dollars. I gave up on the first.

When I made it to the Big Five-Oh on Oct. 15, I discovered that Monday still comes and bills still have to be paid. I have also learned in my first half century that the greatest wealth in life consists in what most folks consider "the little things."

Take, for instance, my hair. I used to pray that my hair would turn gray before it turned loose. However, my brownish locks did both—so now my scalp looks like a shiny, flesh-colored egg covered with strands of salt and pepper. Still, I am thankful that I have hair—it conceals some of the moles on my balding pate.

I am thankful that, in the midst of so many body parts that seem to be breaking down, my nose still works fine. I love the smell of popcorn freshly popped. And of turkey, the mainstay of

Thanksgiving delights. Of a cake baking in the oven. Mmmm. What a delicious fragrance. Eat your heart out, Heaven Sent.

And my ears. Sandra will tell you I am blessed with selective hearing. When East Carolina or the Washington Redskins have the ball inside the 15-yard line, my ears refuse to hear anything but the announcers calling the action. Sandra says I never listen to her. Now, "never" is a pretty strong term. I think what happens is that my ears reach overload before she finishes unloading. I try to listen, but then selective hearing kicks in and—viola—her words become a blur.

Of course, I now need to develop a selective sense of touch because when Sandra is talking to me and my selective hearing engages, she tries to reset my ears with a good poke in the ribs. I never knew that the ears and ribs were connected. Imagine that.

Another thing I'm thankful for: a warm blanket. We have arrived at that awkward time of year when temperatures at night are just warm enough to make me reluctant to turn on the heat—and just cool enough to make me regret that decision in the morning. Nothing seems to cut the chill like being wrapped in blanket—especially when you are cuddling with that someone special—as long as she keeps her elbows to herself.

Sleep is another blessing. Just let me get warm and comfortable and I am apt to nod off just anytime. Which brings up another issue. Why do opposites attract? I am a lark and Sandra is an owl. She loves to hoot way into the night—but she doesn't like to hoot alone. We larks like to get an early start sleeping so we can be bright and chirpy in the morning. If Sandra were a dwarf in the morning, she'd either be Sleepy or Dopey. Past 10 p.m., I become Grumpy.

Now I no longer expect a call from the Nobel Prize committee, Publishers Clearinghouse, or the President with news I've been appointed ambassador to Scotland. Instead, I cuddle with my sweetie inside that warm blanket, breathe in the special aromas of the season, and rejoice in my selective hearing.

So to you and your small blessings—whatever they may be—Happy Thanksgiving.

Christmas brings sorrow as well as joy

When I awakened Saturday morning, I realized that this Christmas would be the first without my dad. I lived with Mom and Dad for the initial 20 years of my life. When I moved to Kinston in 1971 and began adult life on my own, I doubt if a week passed when I did not talk to Mom and Dad on the phone. I talked with Dad more toward the end of his life because his health condition made him housebound, so I knew I could always reach him. That certainty ended September 14, 2000.

Joy is perhaps the most important theme of Christmas. In fact, "joy" is the theme we love to embrace. We play it to the hilt with parties and gift exchanges, with singing and smiles, with calls of "Merry Christmas and a Happy New Year." One of the most famous of all Christmas carols is "Joy to the World! The Lord has come."

If Christ is the center of our Christmas, then we enter into the joy of our faith. If our approach to Christmas is more secular, then we celebrate the joy of hearth and home. Merchants rejoice in the cash register jingle more than they ever did in the tinkle of sleigh bells. Workers take joy in a day or two off the job.

But we tend for forget that sorrow is also a part of Christmas. We forget that our sorrow is often born from the joy we once had. Bob Dylan, one of my favorite songwriters, once intoned, "I can tell you fancy, I can tell you plain: You give something up for every thing you gain. Since every pleasure has its edge of pain, pay for your ticket—and don't complain."

Those of us who have lost loved ones know well that "edge of pain" during special times. Thanksgiving. Christmas. These holidays focus most clearly on family and remind us of the gaps in the family ranks. Granddad. Granny. Granddaughter Caitlyn. Now Dad.

And yet, that "edge of pain" stems from the joy that flooded us in their presence. The greater our joy, the deeper our pain. Time may heal all wounds, but it never fills all the holes left in our lives by the loved ones we lose. Granny died in 1995, but a pang flashes across my memory and soul when I pass her picture or see a thick slice of yellow cake with chocolate icing—the kind she made especially for me.

Because Dad and I were so close, the pain of not being able to wish him a Merry Christmas on the telephone this year is especially deep. The Romantic poetic William Wordsworth wrote: "My heart leaps up when I behold a rainbow in the sky." Wordsworth lived in an era before the telephone, so his experience was a little limited. I am sure my heart has done cartwheels when I hear the voices of certain people on the telephone—Dad, Mom, my children, and good friends. But the things that make our hearts leap can also cause our hearts to drop.

Just a few days after Jesus was born in the stable in Bethlehem, when he was eight days old, Mary and Joseph took him to be consecrated according to their faith. On the way they met Simeon, an old man who had received the promise that he would not die until he saw the Lord's Christ. When this old man took the Christ child in his arms, Simeon praised God with joy. But as Simeon closed his praise and blessing, he turned his eyes upon Mary and offered her a word of warning and consolation: "And a sword will pierce your own soul too."

I am grateful those memories that pierce my soul most often spring from joy. I know others whose souls are pierced by the sorrows rooted in regret—unspoken words that can never be spoken, forgiveness that cannot or will not be extended, and absolution that cannot or will not be sought. These stabs are the most bitter. These wounds, the hardest to heal.

Regret and an unforgiving spirit run counter to the message of Christmas. "Hark! The herald angels sing. 'Glory to the newborn King. Peace on earth and mercy mild—God and sinner reconciled.'" Christmas is a time for reconciliation.

The sorrows I have are sweet sorrows, sorrows born of joy and precious memories. I hope all your sorrows are the same.

However, if some root of bitterness is souring your Christmas spirit, why not do something to make it right? Enter into the joy of forgiveness, of reconciliation, of peace on earth. Enter into the true spirit of Christmas.

Frustrations of fatherhood

Somewhere in the past, clouded in my misty memory, I remember someone saying, "If you want to be a good father, you are doomed to failure."

"What an odd thing to say," I thought as a young dad. But now, as I look back on 27 years of being a father, I better understand the point. No matter how hard a man tries, he can never live up to his ideal of being a "good father" because that ideal is something we fathers carry in our hearts and souls.

Please understand: I am talking only about good fathers. A father is not just the man who sires a child or even a string of children. Procreation does not necessarily make a man a functioning father any more than a wedding ceremony makes him a genuine husband. I gained the office of husband when I said the "I do's" nearly 29 years ago. But since that time, I've had to work at being a good husband.

A wedding ceremony does not magically change a self-centered, egotistical, maturity-arrested boy into a man. Neither does childbirth magically change him into a father. I wish that magic existed. Like everything worthwhile in life, being a good father or good husband takes energy, work, and maturity.

As I look at the four children Sandra and I reared, I often wonder if I was a good father. I tried, but the perils of fatherhood are like landmines strewn along life's path. Did I give them enough of my time? Did I provide enough financial support, enough emotional support? Was I too hard, too soft? Did I nurture them? Did I challenge them? Did I discourage or create self-doubt? Did I hug enough, and wipe away tears enough?

A good father gives of himself to and for his children.

Earning a living and supporting a family is a chief duty of being a good father. But I have known men who were so caught up in this single role that they neglected other fatherly functions. I recall times I lapsed into lie that we men sometimes tell ourselves, the lie that says we are showing our love by the work we do on behalf of our families. After all, I am an American, and we Americans are the hardest working and most productive people among all the industrialized nations.

But children need more than bread and meat, more than roof and bed, more than clothes and car. They need the cool wisdom a father can provide. They need the emotional stability a mature father can lend. They can learn from Dad to develop a rational detachment from their problems so they can examine problems more clearly. They need Dad's time and attention.

I am proud of my children. Sara is a registered nurse. Rachel is an English teacher. Lydia is a commercial graphics artist. Michael, who made the Dean's List during the spring semester, is at East Carolina preparing himself for a career in education. They are all productive, hard-working young people with a sense of self and a strong set of values.

But sometimes I believe they turned out that way in spite of my failings, not because of my fathering. You see, I remember my lapses—the times when they did not really occupy center stage in my world, the times when pressures of work or community involvement or personal pleasure robbed them of my time.

No matter how often my children thank me for what I have done and shower me with their love and devotion, I still feel a sense of frustration and failure because I know I could have—and should have—done more.

Ultimately, the most important gift we ever give our children is our time. A recent survey showed that the average middle-class father believes he spends fifteen to twenty minutes a day with his kids. The key word in that sentence is "believes." The average amount of time each dad actually spent with his kids each day was 37 seconds. Some days I spent zero time with my children. I was up before day and back after their bedtime.

I kissed them goodbye before they awoke and goodnight after they were asleep.

When I was a young man, I had dreams of fame and fortune. I achieved neither. I do not regret those failures. But when I recall the time I robbed from my children, no single regret haunts me more.

Today my three greatest joys are spending time with my wife, spending time with my children and grandchildren, and spending time with my parents. In the final analysis, the investment we make in these human relationships enriches our lives most.

I wish I had invested more.

Food goes fast at concession stand

If I never see the inside of the concession stand at Grainger Stadium again it will be too soon. I did learn two valuable lessons Friday night. First, I have developed a profound respect for folks who work in the fast food industry. Second, when local people sponsor an outstanding tournament, a lot of folks have to work their behinds off.

The ordeal began when my good friend Karl Grant, now my ex-friend, asked if I would be willing to help one of the nights of the 13-year-old Babe Ruth tournament.

"What would I have to do?" I asked.

"Work the admission gate, sell programs, or work the concessions," he replied.

I paused.

"We really need some help," he said.

"Ok. I'll do it."

I should have known that I was in deep trouble when he called and asked if my wife Sandra was coming to help me.

"I don't think she's planning to."

"If you don't want to be working concessions alone, I'd advise you to beg her to help." I've never been one to ignore good advice, so I went into my pitiful hang-dog look until

Sandra said she'd help. We made it to the stadium at 5 p.m. We were each handed a couple of tickets for food and drinks and pointed to the concession stand. An occasional wanderer would come up for a drink or bag of peanuts.

"Do you have sunflower seeds?" someone asked.

Before I could say, "Does this look like a health food store to you?" one of the regular concession workers caught my eye and nodded toward a box of packaged sunflower seeds.

"We certainly do," I said, smiling.

"How much are they?"

The question shook me. Not only did I need to know what we offered, but I also needed to know the prices. I prayed and then found a price list. Prayers are still answered.

"Seventy-five cents."

"I'll take two."

Two more volunteers showed up, Danny and Randy. So we had four volunteers and two Grainger regulars, but almost no business. Sandra and I decided to use a ticket for some supper during the lull. It proved a wise decision. From 5 to 7 p.m. we had a trickle of business.

Around 7:30 someone must have turned on a subliminal neon light flashing, "Eat now! Eat now!" From 7:30 until 10 p.m., we were deluged by people who twisted their way through the concession maze and placed rapid-fire orders for food and drinks.

"I'lltaketwohotdogsaCokefryandalargebagofpeanuts," one guy rattled off.

"Say what?" was all I could manage.

"I'd like a chili dog," another customer said.

"We don't have chili dogs tonight," I said as strains of "Have It Your Way" rushed through my head.

One woman ordered a Coke and popcorn. As Randy drew the Coke, I tried to explain that we had run out of boxes for popcorn, so even though we had popcorn, we had nothing to put the popcorn in.

"I want a coke and popcorn," she repeated.

"But I just explained that we don't have anything to put the popcorn in" I said.

"You mean you're not going to give me any popcorn."

"Bingo!"

"Not going to sell much tonight," she muttered disgustedly as she left.

Oh really, I thought to myself. Why don't you come back here and watch us make this stuff disappear through this window then. I always am decisively clever in silent debates.

As the night wore on, so did my nerves.

"Sunflowers seeds."

"Sorry, we're out."

"Peanuts."

"Out of them too.'

"Hotdogs."

"Ditto."

"Cheeseburger."

"Out of cheese."

"Well, what DO you have?"

"Aching feet, a sore back and a cooler full of candy bars."

"I'll take two Baby Ruths."

"Two Baby Ruths. Hold the aching feet and sore back."

At 10 p.m. the rush hours ended. At 10:15 I was sitting in the grandstand rooting for Kinston as the Grainger regulars cleaned up.

"Going to be here tomorrow?" Chuck Blake asked me.

"You know better than that," I said. "Got to get the Sunday paper out."

For once, I was relieved to have a Saturday job.

CHAPTER THREE

I CAUGHT CRAZY FROM MY KIDS

Inside (the Bathroom)

View of Magic Kingdom and Epcot

Disney World and Epcot Center. Even the names of these places conjure up images of smiling children, awe-struck adults, developing technology, and the timeless merging of past, present and future. I spent a lifetime at Disney World in just two days. Never have so many walked so far in so much heat to stand in so many lines for such a length of time—to do so little.

The trip to the Magic Kingdom began as well as it could with three pre-teen girls, a four-year-old son, a wife, abundant baggage and my abundant self stuffed into a 1979 Ford station wagon—the classic "grocery getter." Actually, I have always been pleased with that car and ignored the taunts from Chevy lovers that F-O-R-D stands for "fix or repair daily." However, near Woodbine, Ga., (surely you have been to Woodbine) my ride "put me down," as the kids say.

Nothing makes me feel more like a fool than bending under the hood, fiddling with wires, and waiting for the water and steam to boil out of the radiator. I don't know why I was fiddling with the wires. I know absolutely nada about automobiles. However, wire fiddling seemed like the right thing to be doing at the time.

"Put the C.B. on Channel 9 and ask for some help," I yelled to my wife over the noise of scores of cars and trucks zooming by. Most drivers looked smug. They had that "Another stupid Tar Heel" look. I've had that glare aimed my way several times while traveling out of state—especially since the University of North Carolina Tar Heels won the NCAA National Men's Basketball Championship in 1982 and N.C. State did a follow up in 1983. We'd all have to carry guns if any North Carolina team had pulled it off again in 1984.

Finally, a deputy sheriff's car crossed the median and headed our way. The deputy stopped, walked toward the car, and asked if he could help. Good, I thought. He looks just like a good ole boy from North Carolina. He even had a pouch of Red Man on the dash of his patrol car.

Before long the deputy was giving my Ford a refreshing drink of cool water. Suddenly, the Ford did a Mount St. Helen's imitation. I glanced at the deputy.

"Still hot," he noted astutely.

The deputy called a mechanic friend who showed up shortly with a tow truck—and a similar pack of Red Man on the dash. I figured they must go to the same church or belong to the same civic club. The mechanic joined us under the hood.

"Most of the time when this happens the thermostat is stuck closed," he said, shifting the wad of tobacco in his mouth. He spat and then lifted a screwdriver, fully 18 inches long, with his left hand, while with the right he hefted a wrench that could have tightened bolts on the U.S.S. North Carolina. He set the screwdriver in amongst the innards of my car.

"Can you fix it?" I asked nervously.

"I'm gonna knock.....!" he yelled just as a huge 18-wheeler blew by a little too close for comfort.

"Your gonna knock my WHAT?" I shouted back.

"That there little center piece outta your thermostat. Then we'll see if the water will run out when we fill up the radiator. If it does, you're okay."

I prayed earnestly that I might see water.

GLUG! GLUG! GLUG! The water went in and the steam came out of the little hole in the thermostat. He hooked up the hose and in a few minutes I was headed toward my brother's home in Orange Park, a suburb of Jacksonville, Florida.

But the trip to Jacksonville was 50 of the longest miles of my life. The car was not overheating, but it had no power. Going up the relatively mild hills on I-95 South, the engine labored and the car's speed dropped from 65 miles per hour to about 40. Something was still wrong with my Fix Or Repair Daily.

Finally, we made it to my brother's house. To make a long story short, three days and $325 for a timing chain and gear later, we were ready for Disney World. One day there convinced me that more car trouble would have been better.

Magic Kingdom

Disney World is 168 miles from Orange Park. The car was running fine, the kids were singing, my wife was sleeping, and I was smiling, nestled behind the wheel. We arrived at Disney's parking lot at 10 a.m.

All the parking sections at Disney World stand as mute reminders of the folly of coming to the place. You can park in a section called "Minnie"—to remind you of the multitudes that enter therein. I don't have to tell you what "Daffy" and "Goofy" suggest.

Disney World is a universe of motion. Trams ply constantly between the ticket plaza and the parking lots. Each car in the tram seats about 30 people, and each tram has at least six cars, so around 180 people climb aboard each tram. Wednesday was going to be a long day. We had to wait for the third tram to make it out of the parking lot.

Why didn't we just walk? The moon was closer. After all, we were parked near the section labeled "Pluto"—not the dog, the planet. No one in his right mind would venture crossing that parking lot without a compass, three days of survival necessities, and a good supply of drinking water. We had none of that. No one is permitted to carry nourishment into the wonderful world of Disney. Besides, the wait for the tram would prove to be the shortest we would have all day.

At the ticket gate we purchased three-day "passports" for four adults and five children. Total admission: nearly $350. [We made this trip in 1985.] After we paid for the passports, we were still nowhere. The passport only allows a person to pass through the gate, wade across a sea of humanity, and stand in line for the monorail to either to Magic Kingdom or Epcot. If you don't like heights, you can arrive at the Magic Kingdom by ferry. If you get sea sick and air sick, save your money.

We walked up the ramp to the monorail for the Magic Kingdom. I felt like an extra for a scene in the Ten Commandments—you know the one—when the Children of Israel go piling out of Egypt. We waited. Monorail after monorail filled up and whisked away. At last, we boarded the monorail and headed to Magic Kingdom. When we arrived, I thought we had missed a stop. We were in another entry plaza and still near nowhere. By this time, the Florida sun snarled down upon us. We walked and walked until we came to Main Street U.S.A. The line stretched from the boarding plaza of the train and Main Street. I was lost in a sea of faces.

I looked around for Gandhi. No luck.

At that moment, we began the systematic visitation of restroom facilities at Magic Kingdom. I did not realize at that point in my life how important—how necessary—how vital— and how wonderful Disney restrooms are. Air-conditioned and no lines. Then, our pattern for the day emerged: Stand in line, go on the ride, and visit the restroom.

"But, Daddy, I don't have to go," my kids told me time and again.

"Shut up and go anyway."

We were in a Marx Brothers' movie—"A Day in the Life of a Bathroom Hopper."

One of the first rides in the park was the Main Street horse-drawn trolley. We boarded in the rain and within minutes the horse existentially expressed my feelings about Disney World. I felt a real oneness with that horse. The relationship was mystical.

Cinderella's Castle was next. Have you ever tried to explain to a four-year-old boy why he can't have that $5,000 collector's sword, complete with case?

Then the Carousel beckoned. I planned to stand beside Michael when he rode the merry-go-round, but when he spotted the empty horsy right next to his, he insisted I RIDE. Unfortunately, it was an inside horse—a small horse...small small—and I am...well...not so small.

Ever see Yosemite Sam on a mule in the Bugs Bunny cartoons?

Michael was happy. I wasn't. After all, I was using a carousel horse as a thong.

"Small World" lay directly in our path. The line did not look long when we joined it. It wound only around and around outside the building. Then we made our way inside the building. I had a flashback. Moses and the Children of Israel were preparing to cross the Red Sea—and all of them were in line ahead of me.

A boat! A boat! My three-day passport for a boat!

"Small World" really is a delight. Boats sail the cool waters of the man-made cavern as little folks from all over the world entertain their Disney visitors. But like most Disney attractions, the length of the ride in minutes seems the same as the length of the wait in hours.

After the ride, we went back to the restroom. I heard voices speaking in five different languages. Although I spoke none of those languages, I understood.

"But, Daddy, I don't have to go," sounded protests in a chorus of varying tongues.

"Shut up and go anyway," fathers from around the world responded.

Bathroom is the universal language.

The Hall of Presidents

Mom and Dad had traveled from Ohio to join us on the Disney excursion. They had visited Disneyland in

California—and loved it. Disney World was another issue. They recommended a visit to the "Hall of Presidents," so we entered the maze and made it into the building where we faced standing room only.

"Where are the presidents?" asked Ginny, my brother's four-year-old.

"Most of them are dead," I replied.

"Did they die here—in the line?" she asked. Children are so perceptive.

What I thought was the "Hall of Presidents" was the waiting room. A sweet voice came on the speakers.

"The Hall of Presidents attraction will begin in eight minutes. Please make your way into the auditorium."

Hundreds began flooding through the doors. Our family joined hands, held on tightly, and hoped we would not end up going over the falls. We made it. We were in the auditorium and began looking around for seats. Every seat was occupied.

"The counters are not working right," a young man informed us. "We will try to bring in some benches." Despite the added benches, Rachel, Lydia and I ended up sitting on the sloping floor. As soon as the show started, we forgot the inconvenience, enthralled by the presidents, their stories, and their speeches. Reality intruded as the show ended and we were herded to the exits to allow the next group of presidential hopefuls to enter the hall.

Lunch time

Finally, we just couldn't put the kids off any longer. They were starving and demanding food. We took them to the bathroom before the meal—and after. An ounce of prevention, you know. Eating at Disney World is an experience in itself. Meals for my family exceeded $20—and that was the economy price. One restaurant we checked offered dining delights to the tune of $12 per person, adult and child. I cringed when I saw the prices. On the way inside, I had accidentally stepped on a French fry.

But at least the restaurant was cool and dark and, for Disney, not crowded. However, all good things must come to an end, and too soon the time came to take our place in the crowds, the heat, and the lines.

We decided to ride the train. A steam-powered locomotive circles all of the Magic Kingdom. Along the way, riders see a burning shack, Deacon Jones and his dog Rufus, some Indians, and a host of other things. The conductor provides continuous narration. The train chugged into the Main Street stop. One of the kids moved.

"Hey! Don't you dare get off this train," I glared.

"But I gotta go to the bathroom," the cherub whined.

"Why didn't you go last time?" I hissed.

"I did," came the meek reply.

"Just wait."

The train started with a jerk (not a personal reference) and off we went to the station at Frontier Land. We pulled in, and the train stopped. For the first time all day, we were not herded away. The crowd waiting for the train was small. My family started disembarking. They paused, looked back at me and asked if I planned to get off.

"Not me," I said. "I'm already on this ride and there's no telling how long it will be before we get on another." We rode the train again—all around the Magic Kingdom. A gentle breeze stroked my face and the smell of summer sunshine filled the air. Too soon, we were back at the station again.

"Getting off this time, son?" Mom asked with a "you'd better if you know what is good for you" edge to her voice.

"I guess so," I replied. "But so far, other than the bathrooms, this has been the best part of the trip."

"I know what you mean," Dad agreed.

Of course, the time had arrived for another restroom stop. When we got to the restroom, the little cherub who just couldn't wait piped up.

"I don't have to go now," she said.

"Oh, yes, you do!" I steamed.

Toward setting sun

The rest of the day followed the same pattern. Finally, we

began making our way toward the monorail and tried to find the nearest position to the exit that would still afford us some view of the famed "Electric Parade," one of the truly remarkable sights in the Magic Kingdom.

People lined Main Street five deep by the time we found some slight area of visibility. We waited. Sandra and the girls climbed on a store's window ledge. When the parade started, I lofted Michael to my shoulders.

The magical, mystery parade began. Creatures composed of lights meandered back and forth in the street. Cinderella was there. Pete and his dragon paraded down Main Street. Overgrown ladybugs, Dorothy and her Oz friends, the Fairy Godmother, and countless others made their way through the streets to the delight of rapt onlookers.

About 40 minutes later, the parade ended and we began moving through the crowd toward the gate. We must have looked like the nine stooges, strung together, clutching hands, snaking through crowds of others who were strung together, clutching hands and snaking around us. At last, the gate. We could see the gate. I felt like yelling, "Thar she blows!" but refrained.

As we passed out of the Magic Kingdom, one of the Disney girls said, "The monorails are not working. Please take the ferry."

"Do what!?" Dad and I said.

I gazed at the crowd. Multitudes of people—thousands upon thousands, and thousands more—huddled toward the ferry dock. The scene reminded me of the Great Judgment Day—the sheep separated from the goats, the saved from the lost. But we kept the faith and, despite the warning, headed to the monorail. We were the sheep. While the crowd of goats still waited for the ferry, the monorail arrived and whisked us back to the parking lot. I bet the goats were still waiting in line when we pulled into our motel.

As we tooled out of the parking lot and away from Disney World, we saw an overpass with a monorail stopped above and lights flashing on the ground below. Only after we arrived at the motel and tuned into the news did we discover that one of the monorails had caught fire. People in the car next to the fire had climbed out of their car and on top of the monorail, edging as far away from the fire as they could get.

In 30 years of Disney monorails, this fire was the first such incident in their history. And we were there to see the tail-end of it. Fortunately, all the people evacuated safely—and no one was injured.

It was a fitting close to our first day.

And the second day—spent at Epcot Center—was like unto the first. I am trying to forget, so I won't bore you with the details. Suffice it to say we visited Spaceship Earth, the World of Motion, and an AT&T Communicorp display, one restaurant, and every restroom, except those in the Showcase of the World.

By 3 p.m. of the second day, we were back at the main gate, debating whether to go back into the Magic Kingdom. A gigantic black thundercloud boiled up behind Magic Kingdom—and was headed our way.

"Let's just go," I pleaded, to the disappointment of my wife and kids—and to the relief of my parents. After a quick stop at the souvenir shop on the way out, a concession I made to assuage the disappointment of all the young and young at heart, we boarded our cars and started out of the parking lot. On the way, the thundercloud burst and rain fell in torrents.

I was smug—and relieved—and glad to be heading home.

Ideal summer vacation

Summer is vacation time for most of us, but the word "vacation" means different things to different people. Some love to trek to the beach where they can do what they would never do at home: endure the relentless rays del Sol—sweating, burning, frying and sizzling. I am amazed at the people I know who spend time here in Kinston running from one air conditioner to the next, trying to avoid the twin whammy of summer heat and humidity, but then head to the beach to get whammed. Maybe salt water makes a difference.

Thinking folks go to the mountains because mountain temperatures are usually 10 degrees cooler than those down here in the flatlands. Of course, your car may get a little steamed climbing those mountains and leave you standing by the side of the road doing the "Hitch Hike."

Vacations are in the eye of the beholder.

For me, a vacation means not having to work. A vacation is being away from incessant phone calls, usually for my daughter Lydia—now that her sisters, Sara and Rachel, no longer live with me. Of course, my son, Michael, is getting his share of calls from Munchkin land.

The telephone ruins a good movie. Friday night I was trying to watch a film I had never seen before—"Dr. Zhivago." I believe RCA put a secret telephone signal inside my VCR that sends out an encoded message, "Call Mike. Call Mike." I end up making more trips to the telephone than to the refrigerator and bathroom put together. So, my ideal vacation means the absence of annoying phone calls.

Reading is one of my supreme joys. So my ideal vacation includes large empty spaces of time that I can cram with reading. In the hours just prior to writing this, I left Gen. Hancock massing his men for an assault on the Confederate salient in what became known as "The Bloody Angle" at Spotsylvania Courthouse, Virginia. I am ready to get the battle underway.

An ideal vacation is one in which I do not feel compelled to spend my time running around to see this and that. Running around takes time away from reading and resting. Resting—now, that's a key part of my ideal vacation. I've never been a person to sleep late in the morning, but I do like to steal away sometimes for a nap in the afternoons.

The ideal vacation must be inexpensive, and that's where I run into the most trouble. Hotels cost big bucks. Eating out can drain a pocket like a thirsty diner drains a tea glass. Gas is not cheap. And please do not take me anywhere that offers books for sale. I am a bibliophile and can justify buying a book easier than my wife Sandra can justify eating out. She'll eat out at the drop of a hat—even if she has to drop it.

I enjoy a view. Waves crashing on the shore have a soothing sight and sound. Mountains rising in majesty and gray mists filling the valleys of the Great Smoky Mountains create awe in me difficult to describe. One day when I have time and money, I want to drive the length of the Blue Ridge Parkway.

The ideal vacation offers a curious mix of family time and time alone. I love to be with my wife and children. We play board games or card games. Sometimes we just talk. Often, we tell the same stories as a way of keeping alive our family's special traditions.

My best vacations have been compromises between activities that please the kids, eating out that pleases Sandra— and quiet time that pleases me. At least none of my vacations end up like a "National Lampoon" vacation. At least, so far.

Proud dad grateful to son

Dear Michael,

I know that I have told you this in the past, but I want to let you know again just how proud I am of you. The latest accolade you have received came from officials of the North Carolina Teaching Fellows program. As you well know, they selected you as a 1999 recipient of the N.C. Teaching Fellows award—a full scholarship that you can use at the school close to our hearts, East Carolina. Your achievement will help ease the financial pressures of seeing you through school. I am grateful to you.

Son, this award is the culmination of all those nights of study—of all those books you read and complained about—of all those math problems you worked, anatomy and physiology charts you memorized, art creations you produced, and places and faces in history you crammed into your head. (I still recall your arguments for naming James K. Polk as this nation's greatest president.)

Remember how I used to tell you needed to do well in school—that if you worked hard and did well, you would be rewarded? Well, your reward came in the mail one recent Friday. I don't think I'll ever forget the look on your face as you tore open that envelope and read the opening words of the letter notifying you of the award. No one had to tell me what the letter said. I could see it in your smile.

I also remember the two months of torment between your finalist interview and the day that package came in the mail. One day you thought you had the scholarship, the next you were unsure, and then you just knew you did not get it. After that, you'd start the whole process again—over and over, moving between confidence to uncertainty and from uncertainty to disappointment, and back to confidence again. I'm glad your agony ended.

To tell you the truth, son, I never had any doubts. You really can't see the young man you have become like I can. I look at you with the eyes of experience that your youth does not afford you. Others see it, too. I remember Mrs. Hunt saying something to me at the Academic Banquet when you became a freshman marshal.

"Michael is really special," she said. Until then, I never really understood that your uniqueness was visible to anyone but your mom and me.

"Michael is so special," Mary Edwards tells me again and again. She loves your openness to her, your consideration, your affection. You have always been special to me since the first day you came into this world—my little boy, my son—and now my young man.

You have so much of life still ahead, so many challenges yet to face: college, teaching, and—one day—a wife and children of your own. I know in my heart that you will accept these challenges with the same determination and work ethic you have developed during your high school years. You never chose the easy path. You took difficult and challenging courses when you could have opted for some easy classes.

You have balanced your academics with music and art and soccer and a part-time job. And you do all of them well.

So I say once again—I am proud of you, son, and so is your mom.

God bless you, and congratulations.

Love,

Dad

Things kids take to college

Saturday was a major milestone in our lives. That's the day Sandra and I got the house back. We moved Michael into a dorm at East Carolina. Of course, tons of his stuff are still at the house and I wonder, after experiencing the leaving home of three daughters, if any of my kids will ultimately get all their stuff out of my house. But that's another story.

What shocked me are the things Michael took to ECU. As we packed him to move, I figured he'd take his clothes, some books, his computer, a radio, and a poster. But as I surveyed his version of "packing," I wondered just what he thinks the college experience is going to be like.

Take his computer, for instance. He wanted a laptop. I advised that he get a desktop with the 17-inch monitor.

"But, Dad," he insisted, "a laptop is much better for a student. I can take it to the library when I have to do research. Also, since I'll have the laptop with me, then anytime I have an idea, I can capture it before it gets away."

"Uh-huh," I said in a tone that proved I was not entirely convinced.

"And in some classes I may even be able to take my notes on the laptop."

Score: Michael 1, Dad 0.

"So you want a laptop."

"That's right. And I want a laptop with a DVD drive, too."

"What's a DVD drive?"

"Well, Dad," he said with the patronizing air only a teen born in this age of technology can muster, "a DVD drive is a new way of storing data. In fact, DVD is far advanced of the old

CD-ROM technology. CD's can hold music, but manufactures can put an entire movie on a DVD disc."

The light broke.

"So, you want a DVD drive so that you can watch movies, is that it?" I said, waiting for the scoreboard to reflect Michael 1, Dad 1. "When do you think you are going to have time to watch movies? You are taking 18 hours. This is the rule of thumb: for every hour you spend in class, you'll spend three hours out of class doing homework, projects, papers, reading and studying."

"Well, I just thought you'd want me to have the latest technology. You know how fast computers go out of date."

Michael 2, Dad 0.

"But I see you have packed your Play Station. Why would you possibly need a Play Station? When are you going to have time to play video games after getting all your school work and watching DVD movies?"

"You don't want me to work all the time, do you?"

"Well...that's sorta what I had in mind. You know: college, education, developing the mind. You could stay home and play video games for free—and I wouldn't have to buy that laptop."

But in my heart, I knew the score: Michael 3, Dad 0.

Just let me give you an idea of what today's college student takes to school. A stereo system, complete with CD player, AM-FM radio and cassette player. A television and VCR. A refrigerator, despite the fact that he has a meal plan to provide 14 meals per week. He doesn't have a microwave yet, but I know that's looming on the horizon. Else how can he heat his mac-and-cheese, oodles of noodles, and pop tarts.

"Son, did you pick up a new dictionary and thesaurus?"

"Not sure I'll need them."

"Do what?"

"Well, doesn't the laptop have a built-in dictionary and thesaurus in the Microsoft Office software?"

I hate it when he is right. Michael 4, Dad 0.

"But, son, most of the time, the dictionaries are fairly limited. You need something like a Webster's Collegiate," I offered weakly.

"If I need one, I'll pick one up on campus."

With that, we loaded his eight pair of underwear, his multitude of shirts, a week's worth of pants, a clothes hamper, his socks, his bathrobe, several single subject notebooks, a single pack of loose leaf paper, some pens and pencils, a box of comic books, some plastic cups and forks, some soap and shampoo, his toothbrush and toothpaste, and other sundries—and we were off.

As I looked around his room at home, I realized that Sandra and I haven't really gotten the house back. I guess the larger-than-life display of Anakin Skywalker gave it away.

Farewell, teen years

Dear Michael,

Beginning today, you leave your teen years and enter the realm of 20-somethings. I have watched with pride as you grew from baby to boy to young man. If I close my eyes, I can see your five-year-old image on the blacktop working so intently to beat me in basketball. You were a fierce competitor—and I had all the advantage. Height. Size. A better outside shot. I determined I'd never let you win. I wanted you to know that your first victory over me was one you earned fair and square. How little I knew. A few months after your first win, I ceased to be any real competition. I retreated to the sidelines to watch you play.

You grew up so fast, son. Some lessons you learned so quickly. I remember reading poems you wrote at 12—poems I envied. You draw like Chuck Jones—I scrawl like an intoxicated chicken. Music was a common bond, but your lead playing left me groping around the fret board while you ran the neck like an Olympic track star.

Twenty years old today. A decade of changes stretches before you that you can't possibly understand. You may hide from these changes a little longer behind the guise of "college boy," but when college ends, adult life begins with a vengeance.

If you think your life changed from 10 to 19, just wait.

In the next 10 years you will enter a career. I hope teaching brings you as much satisfaction as it brought me for so many years. By the time you turn 30, you should be in your eighth year of teaching—established, tenured. But beginning your career will be one of the easiest changes.

Imagine this: During the next 10 years, you are likely to marry. Marriage is nothing like dating. Oh, yes, the sweetness of romance can and should linger in marriage, but keeping that sweetness will be more of a job than I can tell you. Life has a way of wearing you down, preying on your mind, sapping your vitality. The biggest change is ceasing to think in terms of self. Instead, you must learn to weigh every important decision—and most small decisions—based on their impact on two. I can only pray that you won't enter marriage with a parachute. I hope I've raised you to seek a lasting relationship.

Do you ever stop to think that before you finish your 20s you are likely to be a daddy? You will know the excitement and anxiety of discovering that you and your wife are expecting. You'll know the co-mingled thrill and terror of holding your life robed in another flesh. You'll look into a child's eyes and love unconditionally from a depth of soul you never realized you had. Just the way I first looked into your eyes—and continued to look into your eyes until you reached an age when your face was usually averted and your eyes unavailable.

Just remember, before I left my 20s I had three little ones who looked to me for everything, who never worried where the next meal would come from or how the light bill would get paid. I think having you children taught me more about faith than I learned from anything I ever read.

As you traverse the next decade and cope with all these changes, I hope you'll understand that I am here for you. As you well know, I won't intrude. But if you have questions, if your heart aches so badly you can't find anyone to tell, or if confusion fills your mind and you need a sounding board to think things through, then I am here—and will be here for you until my time comes to be buried with my elders.

I have always loved you—and love you now more deeply than ever. But my role is a changing one. Your sisters taught me that lesson. I hope that for each of my children part of my role is to serve as trusted friend.

I have little else to offer but that—but I offer all I have.

Love,

Dad

Tupperware for the college man?

Please try to capture this mental image. I am in my car, Sandra is riding shotgun, as we head to Greenville to attend—of all things—a Tupperware party. Now, add to that image this special location: Son Michael's Greenville apartment.

Michael just completed his sophomore year at East Carolina, so this party is not only going to be at my son's apartment—but at his college apartment. You know what a college apartment looks like? Three guys live there—three messy college guys. As I headed up NC 11, thoughts of attending a party complete with squalor made my tummy begin preliminary hiccup heaves.

No worries, Michael assured me. He would clean up before we got there. Somehow, that thought did not reassure me. I had already experienced his idea of "cleaning up" when he lived at our house. Cleaning his room meant his mom and I thought we could perhaps make out the floor underneath the pile of papers, comic books, magazines, shoes, socks, and assorted clothing scattered by Hurricane Michael. Heading to Greenville, I realized something: the apartment contained Michael times three. My palms began to sweat and my head to swim.

A Tupperware party? Did this boy even know what he had gotten himself into? Now, I knew he wanted to help his mom with a "booking," but did he really think he could order take-out finger foods from the Golden Arches or Burger King? Besides, even if he had recently removed the garbage, wouldn't the fragrance linger on?

When we finally arrived at the party, the floor was straight, and Michael had conned his roommate Thomas into conning his mother into preparing cookies, cake and other delights. Not a single stench assaulted my nose.

Yeah, I thought, but he must have at least seven of us present to get his "hostess" gifts—and to have a truly successful party, he needed to have at least $350 in orders and two bookings. I was sure he wouldn't make the minimum party number, and I certainly had no plans to order $285 worth of Tupperware. I came on this trip to "count" as a party-goer. That's what Dads are for.

As party time approached, Sandra, Thomas, Thomas' mom, Michael and I waited. Precisely at 7 p.m., a knock came.

"Come on in," Michael hollered. The door swung open and in walked three young college women. They took seats on the sofa—the sofa with no legs that rested flat on the floor. Party-goer count: 8—minimum number met and exceeded by one.

The consultant, new to the Tupperware business, enthused about the products she had brought to show us. I had no idea anyone made such a variety of containers. She showed something called a "Forget-Me-Not"—an item used to store half of something—a tomato or onion. But since the "Forget-Me-Not" hangs in plain sight, it is never out of mind.

The consultant had some containers made from the same plastic used to make airplane windshields. She also offered divided lunch dishes, one version complete with a removable tray so if you brought a salad to work, you could nuke the other foods—say your fried chicken and mashed potatoes—without nuking your salad. She promoted pitchers, tumblers, and cereal containers. The consultant kept the pace brisk. Hey, this was more than interesting. It was even fun.

I looked around the room. How in the world could five college students and three parents order enough Tupperware for Michael to make the $350 minimum? How would he get two bookings? At party's end, though, he had his two bookings and about $293 in orders.

"We can delay your total until Friday," the dealer said. Could Michael manage to generate $57 in additional orders by Friday? Michael? Poor college students? Kids who think macaroni and cheese is a balanced diet? $57?

By the time Friday arrived, Michael had $509 in total orders plus his two bookings. He had qualified for two levels of prizes. His mom was happy because he had pulled off a successful party. His sister Rachel was happy as well. Michael was hosting her first party as a new part-time Tupperware consultant.

I shook my head.

Kids.

Just when you think you've got them figured out, they disappoint all your expectations.

CHAPTER FOUR

OF RUG-RATS AND CRUMB-SNATCHERS

A special Christmas

On Christmas Day, as the Parker clan gathered for Christmas dinner, I sat for a while and held the newest member of our family, Caitlyn Faith Dixon. Caitlyn is the child of Sara, my oldest daughter, and Mark, my son-in-law.

Just being able to hold and cuddle little Caitlyn is a miracle because she was not supposed to live more than two months. You see, Caitlyn was born with a genetic problem called Osteogenesis Imperfecta, OI for short. Some folks call the problem Brittle Bone Syndrome. According to her doctors, Caitlyn lacks a key substance she needs to form strong, healthy bones. No medicine can supply what she needs.

Having OI is not Caitlyn's only problem. She has Type 2 OI, the most rare and deadly of all the forms of the condition. Medical authorities say that Type 2 OI occurs because of a spontaneous genetic mutation. The geneticist who examined Caitlyn after she was born told Sara and Mark that Caitlyn would live anywhere from two weeks to two months. Since she was born on Oct. 22, Dec. 22 was a red-letter day for her. On that day she disappointed one of the direst medical predictions she faced.

So far, Caitlyn has constantly proved medical expectations wrong. Doctors told Mark and Sara that Caitlyn would never survive birth—but she did. With Type 2 OI, she was supposed to die within a few weeks from respiratory problems, but just hours after she was born, she was breathing room air—despite the fact that she was four weeks premature. She has had no lung problems yet.

Doctors predicted that she would live no longer than two months because as she develops, her lungs will grow, but her rib cage won't. Eventually, she will go into respiratory distress because her lungs will outgrow her rib cage. Yet, as of Dec. 25, she is growing and thriving, gaining weight. And she is increasing in length—impossible for a child with this severity of OI.

I looked into the face of my little granddaughter as she lay in my arms and prayed for God to continue to preserve her—and to touch and heal her body. I read in the Bible where Jesus touched those afflicted with health problems and made them whole. That's what I pray for Caitlyn—that God would make her whole, even to the point of reordering her genetic structure so that she will be healthy and normal.

Our family has enlisted the support of other people of faith who still believe that God is in the miracle-working business. Sara and Mark attend World Harvest Church in Columbus, Ohio—a church with more than 6,000 members. They faithfully pray for her. One Sunday, more than 4,000 people pledged to forego Sunday dinner and spend that time in prayer for Caitlyn. My brother John attends a huge church in Orlando—5,000 strong—and they pledged their prayer support months ago. Many of my friends around this area have promised to pray for Caitlyn. I am sure they are praying.

I am so thrilled that the gloomy predictions about Caitlyn did not come to pass. I have so many stories to tell her and songs to sing to her. I have so many kisses and hugs to give her. I want to fix bows in her hair, like I did for her mother and aunts. I want to play games with her. I want to let her know just how much her Grandpa loves her.

I covet your prayers for her. Join with Sandra, Sara, Mark,

me, and thousands of others who are praying that God will do a miracle in her little body.

Thanks so much. And I hope your Christmas was as blessed as mine.

'Happy Birthday,' miracle child

Happy Birthday, my darling little Caitlyn.

You are a true miracle—a wiggling, cooing, babbling testimony to the love of God and the power of prayer. Last year when you were born, doctors pronounced a death sentence on you. They said you would live only two weeks to two months. Grandma and I asked people here in Lenoir County to join us in prayer for you. Great-Uncle John in Florida did the same, as did your daddy's family in Pitt County. Great-Grandma and Great-Granddaddy Parker and Mama and Daddy enlisted the support of folks across this country.

We did our best to raise a Prayer Army for you. Tens of thousands of people have made you the subject of special prayer. You wouldn't believe how many people right here in Kinston and Lenoir County still stop me to ask how you are doing and assure me that they are still praying.

Now here you are, a whole year later—still kicking, still cooing, still drooling.

Here we are—still praying, believing, clinging to God's promises.

My little sweetheart, I admire the faith of your Mama and Daddy. They have believed that God will prolong your life and heal your body despite the constant reports of doctors who still say that you are not going to make it. I know it must sometimes hurt them to the heart when they take you in for a check-up. The doctors acknowledge the miracle of your survival but offer no hope that you'll be around to celebrate Birthday No. 2. But Mama and Daddy still believe that God will touch your body and heal you completely of this awful condition—and so do we.

We are praying that one day you can tell folks you

were born with Osteogenesis Imperfecta—Type 2, but that God healed your brittle bones and now you are 100 percent whole. One day, I'll teach you how to spell the name of this condition.

But until the day of total healing comes, we will continue to pray for you and rejoice that the Lord has seen fit to maintain your life. I only wish I could share with folks how sweet you are, and how, despite the limitations of body you endure, you are such a good-natured baby. I wish I could help them see how normally your mind and personality are developing.

What a joy it is just to hold you in my arms, to look into your eyes, to feel your warmth against me, to hear you babble in your foreign baby language. Before long you will make that leap of mind that connects certain sounds to specific objects. "Da-da" will turn into a dictionary of words that will allow us to speak together with mutual understanding.

You have taught us much this year, little miracle girl. We have learned what it means to call our Heavenly Father "Da-da." The Bible uses a little different term: "God hath sent forth the Spirit of his Son into your hearts, crying, Abba, Father." "Abba." "Da-da." Two different sounds for the same child-like trust we must exercise when reason and circumstances try to replace faith with doubt, hope with despair.

As you start a new year, you have so much to learn. A world of knowledge, faith and love awaits you. If you are like your Mama, within the next couple of months you'll be spouting mile-long sentences. Your Grandma and I thought your mama would never stop saying "uh-uh-uh" and pointing at what she wanted. Overnight she seemingly went from "uh-uh-uh" to "Mother, may I have another helping of those delicious creamed potatoes." I bet you'll be just like her.

Great-Grandpa says you love for folks to sing to you. Well, before long you are coming for a visit, so I am practicing some songs—songs I once sang for your Mama, your aunts and Uncle Michael.

Until I can hold you in my arms, I'll just wish you a long-distance "Happy Birthday" and pray for God's continued blessings upon you.

We love you, Caitlyn.

Grandpa

Grandchild home for Christmas

On Thursday I again faced the challenge to "sorrow not as others who have no hope." Sara had called, Sandra told me on the phone, and my precious little Caitlyn had died that morning.

For nearly 14 months, her little body fought a good fight against a congenital birth defect. She lived a year longer than doctors said she would. Thursday morning, Caitlyn just stopped breathing—no fighting, no trauma unit, no flashing lights and screaming sirens, no distraught parents hoping against hope as a medical team worked to save her. She left peacefully.

Sara said that Wednesday night Caitlyn was happy, had a good appetite, and enthusiastically babbled in her baby language. We had called Wednesday morning only to hear Caitlyn fussing to be fed. Sandra even heard Caitlyn call "Mama" clearly. Caitlyn had been "da-da-da"-ing for a while, but even when we saw her at Thanksgiving, she hadn't quite mastered "ma-ma." I'm so thankful my daughter got to hear that sweet sound.

When I called Thursday night to talk to Mark and Sara to offer comfort and assure them of my prayers, their faith was still strong.

"I like to think that she is sitting in Jesus' lap right now," Mark said.

"Caitlyn will have the best Christmas of all of us," Sara said. "We'll be celebrating the birth of Jesus, but Caitlyn is with Jesus."

Home for Christmas, I thought.

I have learned new depths of sorrow. I sorrow that my little granddaughter is gone. The sense of loss is profound. But I have learned a new sorrow—sorrow for my daughter and son-in-law in the loss of their baby. I sorrow for my mom and dad. While Sara and Mark have been in Ohio, my parents often kept Caitlyn for Mark and Sara. Mom and Dad love her deeply.

But in the midst of our deep grief, all of us still have hope. St. Paul wrote to the Thessalonians: "But I would not have you to be ignorant, brethren, concerning them which are asleep, that ye sorrow not, even as others which have no hope. For if we believe that Jesus died and rose again, even so them also which sleep in Jesus will God bring with him."

Our sorrow is tempered with hope because our hope is in the Lord Jesus Christ. We believe in more than life after death. We believe in Heaven after death. We hope in the promise of resurrection. We believe that one day we shall be like the Lord Jesus because we will see Him as He is. Paul told the Corinthians, "to be absent from the body" is "to be present with the Lord." Caitlyn is absent from her body—she is present with the Lord.

Gratitude tempers our sorrow. We had her smiles for 14 months. We had the warmth of her presence for 14 months. We had the joy of holding her, of caring for her. We had the fun of playing "peep-eye," of watching her shake her head when we talked with her and of feeling her small fingers grip our own.

We are also grateful to all of you who prayed for Caitlyn and expressed concern for her and us. Your prayers and concern have been a cloud of witness and comfort, and I cannot thank you enough for rallying to us. May God richly bless all of you.

Death is not the end. Death is a door between two worlds. On this side, we treasure the mortal life we have. But when mortal life ends, we pass into another world. Our prime task is to prepare ourselves to live in both this world—and in the world to come. For those who know Christ, death is just a door into His presence.

Caitlyn passed through that door to her new home.

Home for Christmas.

Courtney joins sister in Grandpa's heart

On Tuesday, Jan. 26, 1999, I became "Grandpa" again.
On that day Sara, my oldest daughter, and her husband,

Mark, became the proud parents of Courtney Faith Dixon—a rambunctious bundle of wriggling energy. Courtney weighed in at 7 pounds, 5 ounces, and was 19 ½ inches long. She has long fingers, big feet, and a head full of brown hair. In short, she is beautiful. I may be a little prejudiced, but she is beautiful.

I didn't want to write about her until I had a chance to meet her personally, which I did a week ago Sunday. She instantly stole my heart. I tried to sneak her back with me when Michael and I had to leave Tuesday, Feb. 2, but Sara and Mark were just a little too quick. They nabbed me with baby in my arms and silly grin on my face. Caught in the act of baby napping. They forgave me, though. They understand my attraction to that tiny creature.

Those of you who know about my precious little Caitlyn understand my ecstasy at Courtney's birth. Caitlyn came into this world with a serious health problem that made her little bones brittle and prevented her from growing at a normal pace. Caitlyn died on Dec. 10, just 12 days before she turned 14 months old. She fought a good fight. She finished her course. And in doing so, Caitlyn helped thousands of people—an army of prayer warriors—to practice their faith. She was home with Jesus for Christmas.

My head and soul took comfort in her departure, but my heart ached. Frankly, my heart still aches when the memory of her smile flashes upon my inward eye. Her physical condition placed severe limitations on her. Most of the time Caitlyn rested in one position, moving only her arms and kicking her feet. Once she was comfortable, she did not like to be moved. I am sure that many times she hurt when we had to move her, but she rarely showed discomfort.

Instead, she bore her afflictions with grace. She allowed us to be close to her, to play with her, to kiss her. Caitlyn enjoyed our attention, and we enjoyed showering her with our love.

But now the crib that was empty is full again. The cry of a newborn replaces a strange, haunting silence. A mother's heart has a new tiny focus of affection. A daddy's smile reigns down again upon a tiny face. And the arms of Grandpa wrap around a new life full of energy and need.

Does Courtney replace Caitlyn? Not at all. People are not interchangeable like parts of a car. Each child is special—one of a kind. Caitlyn will always have her special place in our hearts. Her antics etched deep memories in our minds and souls. Those marks abide. But Courtney is doing some etching of her own. She is making her own special marks within each of our hearts. In so many ways, she is following the trail that her big sister blazed when Caitlyn found her way into the permanent recesses of my inner being. And although these two little girls will never meet in this life, I hold both of them close together in my heart.

A PERSONAL NOTE: My family and I appreciate so much the cards, letters, phone calls and personal words of comfort and support during this time of loss of our little granddaughter, Caitlyn. Although I have been known to turn a good phrase at times, I really cannot find the words to thank you for your love and concern. May the Lord richly bless each and every one of you.

Grandchild kindles memories

I spent last week visiting Courtney Faith Dixon—my little granddaughter. In a couple of weeks, she will be six months old. Of course, she needed less than six seconds to win my heart when I had my first chance to see her in late January. I spent only a few hours with her then. We made one of those quick trips, spending as much time traveling as we did visiting. But when a new grandchild makes an appearance, distance and fatigue just don't matter.

This past week was a different story. When we landed at Port Columbus (Ohio) International Airport, daughter Sara was waiting when we deplaned—and so was Courtney. I walked to them. After I said a quick hello to Sara, I told her I'd be glad to carry the baby. In less time than it takes to say "Grandpa," Courtney was in my arms.

Now, I shared her with Grandma and Uncle Michael, too. I don't want you to think I monopolized Courtney. Every now and then, we'd even let a parent or great-grandparent hold her. Courtney visited every day, so between naps, bottles, and diaper changes we had time to play and cuddle.

I generally get fretted when I hear women-folk dissect a baby's features—nose like Uncle Joe's, mouth like Granny Susie, forehead like Dad, ears like Mom—as if a baby was a patchwork quilt of some sort.

But looking into Courtney's eyes took me back 26 years to Sara's birth. Sara was born at the old Lenoir Memorial Hospital here in Kinston. During that time doctors looked on daddies as filth-infested vermin that needed to be kept at a safe distance from mothers and babies. A stocky nurse arrived from delivery.

"Mr. Parker?"

"That's me," I said.

"Here's your baby girl."

The nurse removed the blanket that served as a veil covering a face with chubby cheeks and closed eyes. Now, I know some of you will not believe what I am going to say next. As I looked down at my baby girl, I thought, "Man, she looks just like a frog."

But then Sara opened her eyes, and I was in love. Deep eyes. Blue eyes. Deep, deep love. Her frog-like features disappeared. She was beautiful. I can close my eyes and see those deep, blue eyes even now.

I saw them again—with my eyes open—as I looked into Courtney's eyes. A new generation of deep blue. A new ocean waiting for visions only experience can supply. I have no idea whose chin, mouth, ears, forehead, neck, or fingers she has. But her eyes are her Mom's.

That experience more than any other confronts me—and comforts me—with the reality of the continuity of life. Just like her Mom, Courtney fights sleep, loves to stand up in my lap, and responds to music—even to my singing.

After Sara was born in November 1972, we made a Thanksgiving trip to my grandmother's house in Vinton,

Virginia. My mom and dad drove from Columbus, Ohio. They left after Dad got off work and arrived about 5 a.m.—just in time for Sara's first feeding of the new day. Dad snatched Sara and bottle away from Sandra and undertook his first grandfatherly task. After Sara finished eating, Granddad burped her. Then Sandra changed her, and Sara was ready for her morning nap.

I looked into the bedroom and saw my dad asleep with his hand hanging inside the bassinet. I peeked over the side. Sara's small fingers curled around one of Dad's. Now I understand what pushed him and Mom to drive through the night instead of waiting to leave the next morning. They were drawn by the tug of a grandparent's love.

Haley brightens Grandpa's sky

I am sure most of you have heard of Halley's Comet, the vagrant dirty snowball that hangs around our solar system and puts in an appearance about every 76 years. After I saw a photo of its 1910 appearance, I hoped I would live until 1986 for its next return. After all, I was about 10—no, not in 1910—and 1986 seemed two lifetimes from 1960. I would have to live to the ripe age of 36. By then I would be an old man, my 10-year-old perspective told me.

I did manage to make it to 36 after all, but the comet's last visit was a bust. The comet had none of the breath-taking brilliance in the night sky that marked the 1910 visitation. I doubt I'll be around to see its return in 2062 AD—at least, not in this world.

But now a new Haley brightens Grandpa's eyes. She made her first appearance at 9:23 a.m. Thursday—a 6-pound, 12-ounce bundle of wiggles and insatiable hunger. Her complete name is Haley Faith Dixon. Mama Sara is doing just great, resting up from the delivery, and Daddy Mark is still recovering from near-terminal happiness.

Sandra and I went to visit Sara and Haley in the hospital. We took Courtney with us so Courtney could have a chance to meet her little sister. Courtney is 13 months old, so I wasn't really sure what kind of reaction she would have to Mommy holding another baby. Courtney showed interest but no jealousy. Of course, I had to snap some photos of Sara, Haley, Courtney and Grandma Sandra. Then Sara handed Haley to me so she could hold Courtney for a while.

Now, during the past 13 months I have been able to hold Courtney numbers of times. Being able to hold her close and cuddle her thrills me, no matter how many times I do it. But somehow holding a newborn grandchild always makes the event special. What can match gazing into the face of your child's child?

My child's child. Only yesterday we brought Sara home from the hospital. By the time you read these words, Sara will have brought Haley home. In what will seem like a day or two, Sara will look into the eyes and face of her child's child.

What bonds can be more real, more vital, than the bonds of family? Neither Haley nor Courtney had to do a single thing to earn my love. I love them because I love their Mom.

As I looked into Haley's little face, I saw a bit of my Granny, Lady Belle Parker. Haley seems to have Granny's smile. I sat amazed at how traits seem to span the generations. Just how does Granny's smile show up five generations later? Oh, I know the basic concepts about DNA and realize that these strands of life-stuff replicate time after time. But, still, to see a smile on my granddaughter's face that I used to see on my grandmother's filled me with awe.

As I sat in the chair, holding Haley close, I thought about my mom and dad. They haven't seen Haley yet, and until Sara and Mark can take their family to Ohio, they won't. Mom and Dad used to care for Courtney when Mark and Sara lived in Ohio. They had the privilege of holding and loving their great-granddaughter. Mom and Dad love me, and that love passed to Sara and to Courtney. Love reaches across years and spans the generations.

So now instead of hoping to see 2062 and the return of the dirty snowball, I have a new hope. I want to live long enough to cradle Courtney's and Haley's children in my arms, look into their faces, discover what traits they carry from me, Sandra, my Mom and Dad, Granny. I probably won't make it to 112 to see the comet's next return, but if I can hold on until 75 or 80, seeing my great-grandchildren is one dream that could well come true.

Lessons grandkids teach

One Saturday evening, after granddaughters Courtney and Haley had spent the day with us, I looked around the house. We had just gotten the little ones to sleep. Next thing I knew, Michael and his girlfriend Jimmi (they had come to "see the babies") were stretched out on the couches, asleep. Rachel, who had helped provide childcare, was asleep on the bed in what is now called "Haley's room." Of course, Sandra and I were present and accounted for, as well. Sandra, too, was asleep. I laughed to myself as I collapsed in a chair. Two babies. Five adults. All exhausted.

Babies can wear you out. When they want something, they want it NOW. When they need something, they need it NOW. Of course, at the time, neither Haley nor Courtney could talk beyond Courtney's "Da-Dee" and "Mom-Mee," so they couldn't tell us want they wanted. Instead, we played the guessing game. I am sure that parents and grandparents reading this will understand what game I'm talking about.

All is quiet, and then the storm hits. A baby howls nearby. Startled, we check for blood and broken bones because we are convinced that only some life-threatening injury could provoke such a sound. Since we can't find a broken bone or bleeding, we begin the checklist. Check diaper. Check hunger. Check fever. Begin toy check—offer the teddy bear, the lamb, the little alligator, the ball, the book, the red block, the green block, the blue block…Wait. That was it. Courtney wanted the blue block.

Of course, Courtney didn't bother to look at the blue block. She raised her eyes heavenward as she emitted her cry.

Why didn't she just crawl over there and get the block herself, I wondered.

That point brings us to Lesson Two about babies. Babies know instinctively that they enter this world as royalty. I'm not talking about that cheap kind of royalty either. Babies are not dukes or earls or countesses. They all are crown princes and princesses. While logic might suggest that if the baby is a prince or princess, then the parent must be a king or queen. Nothing is further from the truth. In the baby worldview, adults exist for a single purpose—to serve baby's every whim. Adults are the serfs of the realm. So when Courtney wanted the blue block, her cry represented a form of noblesse oblige.

That day, two babies had five adults scurrying to meet their every desire. Now and then, Haley would allow us to cuddle her just a little, a royal favor granted for services rendered. Courtney is not a cuddle baby, so the closest thing we get to a royal favor from her is a smile or giggle.

Time darkens the true memories of baby's first words, so allow me remind you. The order of words a baby learns to say with understanding is: Daddy, Mama, No, Eat, Me, My, Mine. If you want to discover the true center of the universe, just find a baby. They are born knowing that all creation revolves around them. Of course, two babies means two universes on a collision course. Let me tell you, the Zen riddle "What is the sound of one hand clapping" pales when compared to deeper Zen of this baby riddle: "What is the sound of two universes colliding?"

Did you know that both my granddaughters entered this world knowing the facts of life? Ice cream tastes better than broccoli. Water is a poor substitute for something to drink. Milk may be filled with calcium, but ice tea will give you a caffeine jolt. Cheerios can cut the edge from an appetite, cure baby-blues, and keep an adult busy doling them out to you. My grandkids have also demonstrated that adults are highly trainable.

Babies are wired into the energy force that powers the universe. Compared to Courtney and Haley, the Energizer Bunny moves in haltingly slow motion. Bunny is a 1962 VW beetle. Haley and Courtney are dragsters. For instance, let's say that Haley is moving toward whatnots that she knows she is not supposed to bother. Before I can even complete saying, "No," she has grabbed the whatnot, examined it, polished it, and turned to crawl away with it. I mean, how much time elapses between "N" and "O"? Evidently, in a baby's mind, "No" is the universal command to cry.

"Haley, no."

"WAHHH!"

Well, Courtney and Haley will continue their research program on me. They are planning to write a treatise titled something like: "Grandfathers: Developing a Consistent Methodology for Training and Domination." I'll try to keep you posted on how they are progressing.

Grandpa yet again

At 4:48 a.m. on Monday, April 2, 2001, the telephone rang. Of course, I was dead asleep and had to fumble to find the phone.

"Mumhprme," I muttered into the phone because my brain hadn't quite connected with my vocal chords.

"Mr. Parker, Sara just had the baby. A little girl. Taylor is here," said Mark, my son-in-law. "She and the baby are both doing great. They haven't weighed her yet, so I don't have that information. I just wanted you to know she's here."

Somewhere between "Sara" and "just had," I received an adrenaline jolt that turned me from groggy to instantly alert—something akin to washing down two No-Doze with a cup of Expresso.

"Sara and the baby are doing OK?" I asked.

"Both are doing great." He had to go make a couple of other calls.

"Do we have a baby?" Sandra asked.

"Yep. You're Grandma again."

For the record, Taylor Faith Dixon entered the world at 4:

39 a.m. on April 2. The tale of the tape: six pounds, 10 ounces, 19 inches long. Sandra was scheduled to go into work at 12:15 p.m., so she made a morning trip to see Sara and Taylor. She called me later that day.

"She is so beautiful," Sandra gushed. I knew Sandra was looking at that reddish, writhing thing with eyes only a mother or grandmother has. Most of you have seen a newborn. For lack of a better term, a newborn looks, well, under-inflated most of the time. My daughter Rachel, who visited Taylor and Sara Monday evening, says she believes they have only one newborn picture—and that they pass it around over and over again. On Tuesday, Sandra and I both went to visit them—and Taylor is beautiful. I have the evidence on videotape.

I had forgotten how small a newborn baby is. I've heard mothers describe the birthing process as trying to push a bowling ball through a garden hose, so I know when a mother is giving birth, a baby does not feel small. I wasn't as big as a bowling ball when I was born, but I did weigh in at eight pounds, two ounces. I was more like a cannon ball. My brother, John, was closer to bowling ball weight at an even 10 pounds.

As I held Taylor at the hospital, I had to do a body check. Do all grandparents do that? I looked at Taylor's little hands to make sure Mark hadn't added any unusual genes to our pool. Four fingers and a thumb on one hand—the same on the other hand. At least that part of the gene pool is intact.

Taylor has the longest fingers I've ever seen on a baby. She has a tiny palm with skinny, spidery fingers that stretch out and wriggle. They are strong, too. I did the "Grab Grandpa's finger" test [no, it is not the same as the "Pull My Finger" trick]. She has a good grip. Her little arms are barely as big around as one of my fingers.

Saturday evening, Mark and Sara brought Taylor, Courtney and Haley for a visit. I played with Courtney and Haley for a little while, but toward the end of the visit, it was Taylor time. Sara had just fed her and asked me if I wanted to hold her. Was that a trick question? So I took my tiny granddaughter and placed her on my ample tummy. She snuggled in for a nap. She was so warm and so light as she folded into the fetal position she practiced for nine months.

I looked at her sisters. A little more than a year ago, I was holding Haley the same way. Now Haley is up, walking, mumbling in her baby talk, and scattering books and toys all over the living room. Miss Courtney was prissing around, a big sister with necklace and bracelets, straightening Haley out when she got out of line. Courtney turned two on January 26. In January 1999, I was holding a newborn Courtney, marveling at how petite she was. Then I think, shortly after November 14, 1972, I was holding their mother, my little Sara—amazed at how anything so small at six pounds, five ounces could possess so much beauty.

They start so small—they grow so fast. Before Sara knows it, she'll be holding her grandchild. That time, 20 years or more hence, seems so distant to her right now. But before she knows it, that time will be here.

I hope I am around to see it.

Putt-Putting with Papa

First things first: I am Papa, a word pronounced with two distinct, equally weighted syllables. The word is not "PA-pa" nor is it "pa-PA." In Courtney-speak, the correct pronunciation of my title is "PA-PA." My two-year-old granddaughter has given me a name I know will spread among all my grandchildren.

Second things second: putt-putt is a form of golfing suited to people, such as me, who have no desire to walk miles chasing the little white pill of great price. Goldsboro has a twin putt-putt course, the locale of this story.

Our weather had just snapped out its throwback to winter. The sun was visiting, and a gentle breeze wafted. Sandra and I played host to Sara, Mark, step-grandson Jonathan and the three grandgirls—Courtney, age 2; Haley, age 1; and Taylor, age about one month. Rachel and son-in-law Toby joined us from places east. After we finished eating at the Sandpiper, someone had the wonderful idea to do a little early birthday celebration.

I am always pleased when any of our kids take time to visit us, but one thing you need to understand about grown-up kids is that getting a significant portion of them together at any given time is a rare event. Remember how busy your life was in your mid to late 20s? In fact, I've done some mathematical calculations and developed a formula that gives the odds of grown kids visiting at the same time. Number of kids visiting raised to the power of number of kids visiting. For instance, we have four children. If one of the kids visits, then we have one raised to the first power—which is one. However, if two kids come calling, then we have two kids raised to the second power, which is one in four.

The chance of all four of our kids coming at the same time is four raised to the fourth power—or one in 256. If you are confused, just give me a call and I'll calculate your personal odds based on the number of your kids.

We had two kids present, a one-in-four chance of that occurrence. Sons-in-law and grandchildren don't figure into the total because sons-in-law generally go where they are instructed to go—and so do grandchildren who have not reached driving age.

Since May 1 is Sandra's birthday, and since Rachel knew the odds of kids being present on that day were slim, she suggested the putt-putt. So here we were, heading to Goldsboro to enjoy the unadulterated pleasure of being together.

So now we are back to "second." I paid for a group ticket before either of my sons-in-law could reach for their wallets. The fellow behind the counter began distributing clubs and golf balls. We obtained small versions of something that looked like a cross between a golf club and a hockey stick. These baby clubs were also blaze orange, a fact that did not escape my notice. Clubs and golf balls in hand, we headed to the first hole.

Mark placed Courtney's ball on the dimple that serves as a tee and instructed her in the proper use of the club. She swung once, missed, and then kicked the ball, running and chasing it to the hole. By the time the ball stopped rolling, she lined up the club—and knocked the ball backward. With the nonchalance of a two-year-old, she picked up her ball and dropped it in the hole. She retrieved the ball and headed for hole No. 2.

While Courtney was scoring somewhere from one to 12 on the first hole, depending on how many times you count kicks as strokes, Haley was carrying her orange golf-club hockey stick around on her shoulder as she held the ball in her hand. I teed up and hit a beautiful shot that just lipped out and came to rest six inches from the hole. The next thing I knew, Haley snatched my ball and headed to hole No. 2. She didn't even mark the spot.

Mark raced behind her, retrieved the ball, and, as Haley complained loudly, placed the ball back on green one somewhere near the spot it had come to rest prior to what Toby dubbed "the Haley Hazard." My golf card said, "Pro, Par 2" and "Amateur, Par 3." I now knew that each hole was closer to a par 4. Haley Hazard.

Of course, the Haley Hazard was not always in effect because sometimes she wandered to a nearby location to watch water trickle or a leaf skip across the lawn. Then, sometimes she found an object, like the cap of a drink cup, to put in her mouth.

"Dirty, dirty," I told her as I gently removed the cap from her grip. Her brow furrowed, her lips curled down, but the storm in her face passed before it grew to wail force. Then she smiled and tried to insert her entire golf ball into her mouth.

Papa putt-putted the longest 18 holes of his carpet-golfing career. (And so did Grandma.)

'Action Jaxen' enters our world

I have a little help writing today, so please excuse whatever "editorial intrusions" come your way. My wife Sandra insisted on occupying a seat right beside me so she could offer her observations about the latest blessed event in the Parker family.

At 3:47 p.m. on Monday, April 15, Jaxen Parker Wood made

his opening appearance at the Birthing Center of Raleigh's Rex Hospital. Jaxen is doing well. We last saw Mama Lydia and Daddy Robert tip-toeing across the clouds. I figure a couple of 2 a.m. feedings will bring them crashing to earth. Jaxen weighed in at seven pounds, four ounces. When he stretches himself to full length, he is 21 inches. We have already dubbed him Action Jaxen.

"And he is so sch-weet," Sandra just cooed in my ear.

"But, honey, 'sch-weet' just doesn't fit AP style. If you are going to contribute comments to this column, you must speak in AP style."

"Sch-weet is da word, is da word, is da word," she is singing to the tune of the title song from "Grease." How will I ever know if she loses her mind?

I first met Jaxen on Tuesday. He more closely resembled one of the Seven Dwarves—Sleepy—than Action Jackson of movie fame. I saw him in the hall just before they took him for a "procedure," as the nurse delicately called it.

Later I discovered what the "procedure" was. Without violating medical confidentiality, let's just say that Jaxen's procedure could have qualified him to enter into God's covenant with Abraham. I cringed.

No wonder guys have such a warped vision of life. I mean, here was this little fellow, not even in the world 24 hours, and already someone had smacked him on the butt and trimmed... well, you know.

When we paid Jaxen and parents a visit Saturday, Jaxen was in action. I hadn't really heard him cry, so I was not expecting the wave of sound that came crashing from his small mouth. Jaxen flung his mouth wide, showed his tonsils, and let rip with a volume that would make an operatic tenor envious. If Ziggy Marley is thinking about reforming his dad's old group, Jaxen would definitely fit as a Wailer.

Jaxen has already seized control. He cries and Lydia jumps. He has established his pattern: cry, eat, nap, cry, eat, nap. Just like his Grandma Sandra, I said to myself. If we just substitute the word "complain" for "cry," they are perfectly matched.

(Excuse me a second. I need to wait until my eyes can focus. I forget Grandma Sandra was reading along. After she read that last paragraph, she whopped me upside the head. Glad she didn't have a rolling pin handy.)

The women are already playing the "parts" game. Jaxen has Robert's ruddy brown hair, Lydia's long, graceful fingers, and—according to Grandma Sandra—my lips. The lips issue is not quite settled. Some claim Jaxen has Robert's lips, but Sandra disputes this notion.

Frankly, I have my suspicions about her comparisons between newborns and me. She told me Jaxen "looks just like" me. When I saw him, I immediately saw the resemblance—thin hair, chubby cheeks, and wrinkled face. Please remember: she also told me that Courtney, Haley and Taylor all "looked like" me when they were first born.

Thanks goodness they have lost their "resemblance" to Papa.

And I am sure Jaxen will come into his own before long. As he does, my lips may be all he retains from the contribution I made to his gene pool.

I'll keep you posted.

CHAPTER FIVE

THE GLORY OF CHILDREN
"Children's children are the glory of old men; and the glory of children are their fathers [and mothers]." Proverbs 17:6

Love reaching across the years

Sandra showed me a paper she had found. Folds creased the pages cutting so deeply that the paper nearly fell into eight small pieces. The cream-colored sheet showed signs of dark stains ranging from gray to brown. I caressed the page until it lay flat on a lap table and squinted to make out the faded words:

"Pearl Harbor was bombed / December seventh nineteen forty-one / Just one year from that day / My husband was called away / The seventh of December nineteen forty-two / He was carried to Fort Bragg to see if he would go through. / He passed—got a seven-day furlough—/ On December fourteenth he had to go."

As I read, my inner ear began to sound the rhymes. At first, I had not noticed the rhymes because I was trying so hard just to make out the words on the page. But after another four or five lines, I looked at Sandra.

"It's a poem," I said.

"It is?"

"Yes. Look at these rhymes." I read the end rhymes, and Sandra saw the pattern. Her eyes glistened. Mine did too. We realized that we were reading a poem Sandra's mother Rebie wrote to Sandra's father after he left for World War II.

Floyd Dawson entered the U.S. Army on Dec. 14, 1942. He was assigned to a training base in Colorado to prepare for cold-weather warfare. After seven or eight months, he shipped out to the Pacific theater, where he served in India and helped build the Burma road. So much for cold-weather training.

Floyd served chiefly as a medic with 13th Mountain Medical Battalion. I have searched for some information on this outfit, but so far I have found nothing to give us any idea of just where he went and how he served. I do know that when he returned from the war in December 1945, he also returned to the home and the soil. He labored as a farmer until his death in 1969. Rebie never remarried.

As we studied that folded sheet of paper, we came to understand the meaning of the stains. Floyd had carried the love poem with him as he served during the war. The discolorations were stains from his sweat.

"When he left to go / I knew it wasn't for just a day or so / I came home from taking him off / I walked through the house, somehow I felt lost / I tried to be brave. I didn't cry, / Not even when we kissed good-bye / We were both so brave. I prayed to God to help me do splendid / Till this cold-blooded war would soon be ended."

When Floyd left Colorado to go overseas, Rebie was expecting a baby. That baby came on May 1, 1944. That baby is now my wife, Sandra. She was 18 months old before her daddy had the chance to see her.

Rebie closed her poem by signing her name: Mrs. Floyd L. Dawson, and then she added a note beneath her name:

"I will always love only you, my dear sweet darling. Some day soon we will be together to stay for always. No one will ever take your place, darling. All of me belongs to you, sweetheart."

Miles separated them then. Years—and death—separate them now. But the love they shared is as clear today as it was that day more that 50 years ago when she touched pen to paper to create a rhyming record of her devotion to him...and to express her hope that soon the war would be over and they would be together once again.

May your love be as lasting on this Valentine's Day.

My role model

Since yesterday was Father's Day, I want to spend some time praising the man who had the single greatest impact on my life—my dad, Henry Parker. I just made a trip to visit with Dad, Mom, my daughter Sara, son-in-law Mark—and little Caitlyn, my miracle grandchild. Today she is eight months old and still going strong.

When I get to Ohio for a visit, I spend a great deal of time just sitting and listening to my father. I just can't seem to get enough of his voice—and of his wisdom. How odd. When I was growing up, I dreaded listening to my father drone on and on. I told him once when I was a teen, when we were both in good moods and I was out of range, that he ought to record his lectures and make me listen to the taped versions. Like tape 37—the "when I was a boy and walked through snow to get to school" lecture. Or Tape 119—with the theme "do it good, do it all, do it well or not at all." (And Dad thought I didn't listen.) All those stories—over and over again. I used to wonder when he'd ever get some new material. Now I look forward to hearing those old, old stories. I finally realized what powerful teaching tools they were and are.

I learned valuable lessons from my dad. Lesson No. 1: "If your word is no good, then you are no good." Despite the con artists and truth-twisters so prominent today, I have tried to practice this lesson. When Dad gave his word, his word was sacred bond. I have never heard anyone accuse my dad of misleading anyone or lying to anyone. I have seen him go out of his way, at great sacrifice and inconvenience, to do what he said he would do. When many, perhaps most, would have offered an excuse for failing to keep their bond, Dad just kept his word. No excuses.

I learned the value of education from both my mom and dad. Dad especially valued education because he quit school at the end of the ninth grade. He knew first hand the troubles he suffered because he lacked a high school diploma. He and my mom determined in their hearts that both their sons would graduate from college—and my brother John and I both graduated from The Ohio State University.

My dad taught me to treat all people fairly. Although he grew up in a time steeped in racism, my dad accepted all people, regardless of skin color, ethnic background, or nationality. When he worked as a shop foreman, he gave many hours after work to help apprentices learn to do sheet metal work—the trade he loved. He never made a difference between white and black apprentices. His only rules were do your best work and learn your trade well.

Dad modeled for me how to be a good father. I can't say that I always got along with him when I hit those stormy teenage years. I took my trip over fool's hill. When I got to the other side, I discovered that Dad already knew what was on that other side. He tried to tell me, but I was not wise enough to learn from his mistakes, so I had to learn from my own. He was fair, firm and strict as a disciplinarian. He taught John and me to tell the truth, no matter how much we dreaded the consequences. We knew that whatever punishment was in store would be worse if we lied. He taught me how a father gives of his life's energy to provide for his family and of his love to nurture his wife and children.

Dad modeled how to be a good husband. He and my mother were a team. They agreed in matters of discipline, and they agreed in matters of money. They worked together to rear a family, to conduct their business in an upright way, and to secure their part of the American dream.

On this day after Father's Day, I want to acknowledge his influence on me as a man, as a worker, as a father, and as a husband. I count myself blessed to have a father who loved me and cared about the man I would become. I have tried to return the favor to my children, but only time will tell if I have come close to the standard Dad established. I hope I do.

A mom who deserves honor

In all the things I have written about my family, I have had the hardest time trying to write about my mom. Every time I stare at my computer screen to write about her, my mind seems to grope for the right words to capture her essence. But as Mother's Day approached this year, I decided to try again to tell you how wonderful she is.

My mom, Irene Parker, is the hardest working person I have ever known in my life. She can get more work done accidentally than most people accomplish in their most serious exertions. She works hard as a homemaker. She worked hard at being the mother of two sons. On every job she has ever held, her supervisors always praised both her work effort and her performance.

She established this work ethic early in her life when she grew up in the second batch of kids in a family of 13. Mom was the oldest of the second group. She was the one who cooked meals, cleaned house, and washed clothes to assist her mother, who tended the garden, milked the cows, and did hundreds of other jobs that a farm wife must do.

Mom knew the pangs of poverty. She grew up in one of the poorer sections of West Virginia where a grown man would cut brush from daybreak until dark for 50 cents a day. But her limited economic resources taught her to value the truly important things in life —like honesty, compassion, and the knowledge of right and wrong. She has never fallen into the trap of material things.

When Mom realized that Dad's health was growing worse and that his working days were coming to an end, she took a job outside her home for the first time since she became a mother. Early in their marriage, Mom had worked outside the home, but from the time I was born until my brother was a high school junior, Mom was a full time wife and mother. With Dad's health in decline, she took a job to help get the house paid off early and to clear their few debts.

What I most remember about Mom as I grew up was her concern that I would do my best. I am ashamed to say that I was not an industrious student. I had to stop telling my children how well I did when I was in school after Mom gave me copies of some of my old report cards. I was never in any danger of failing, but I just never worked to my potential. My lack of effort was not Mom's fault. She worked with John and me on homework. She drilled us in spelling. She checked our math. She attended PTA meetings and parent-teacher conferences. She wanted us to excel, to take advantage of opportunities she never had.

And she showed us love. She loved me enough to discipline me when I got out of line. She loved me enough to keep my dad informed when I did wrong. Mom and Dad never used John or me as pawns in the power games that some parents seem to play. They had a solid front when it came to their sons. She and Dad did not send John and me to church—they took us to church. We were there every time the doors cracked open—even at times when nothing was going on for adults. I have seen Mom read her Bible and pray, but I have never seen her watch a single episode of a soap opera.

During these past few years when Dad's health has limited what he can do for himself, Mom has increasingly taken up the slack to make sure that he lives in comfort. She helps him bathe, makes sure he takes his medicines, and encourages him to eat well and exercise.

Irene Parker is woman who shows love through her actions. She firmly believes that "Pretty is as pretty does." She is a living illustration of what James the Apostle meant when he said, "I'll show you my faith by my works," as she translates scripture into practical living.

Dad loses battle but gains eternity

Thursday morning I watched my father, Henry Parker, die. He had been in the hospital for a week as we waited for a hole in his lung to close. Since Dad suffered from asbestosis and emphysema for more than 30 years, we knew his chances of recovery were slim. We nurtured hope as long as we could hope that somehow he would snap back from this problem as he had done from past bouts with respiratory problems.

But around 3 p.m. Wednesday, he changed for the worst. He gazed straight ahead with an expressionless stare. We could not get him to respond when we called him or tapped his arm and shoulder. His doctor came in and checked him.

"He might come out of this," the doctor said. "I've seen it happen. But frankly, I don't expect him to make it through the night."

We started the vigil that we knew would end only when Dad took his last breath. His body struggled for nearly 10 hours to keep its tenuous hold to life, but the evidence of impending death grew stronger. Mom was with him, as were my brother John, my wife Sandra, and my daughter Rachel. Two friends, Don and Judy Brammer, helped us keep watch until 12:30 p.m.

"The last thing to go is their hearing," a nurse told us. "Talk to him. He can still hear you."

So we talked. We shared memories. We laughed. We cried. I even sang a few songs for Dad—songs of faith, songs of hope. As we talked, we took turns holding his hands and brushing his forehead. I hoped he could sense the love behind each touch and each word. Ten hours is a long time to say good-bye.

As the end approached, we checked his blood-oxygen concentration. When he first became unresponsive, his level was 95 percent, but toward the end, it had dropped to 63. I checked his pulse and felt only a hint of a heartbeat. He breathed in deeply—then out. Then he took one more deep breath—and he was gone.

I felt so relieved that his suffering was over. I thought of the words of Paul the Apostle: "I have fought a good fight, I have finished my course, I have kept the faith." Dad had done all of those. He left to receive his eternal crown of life.

But relief mixed with sorrow. All of us who kept that sad vigil—and all of those who were in other places waiting, praying—understood we had lost one of our most precious treasures. Dad was a treasure in an earthen vessel, but at 12:55 am Thursday, only the vessel remained with us. His soul was with the Lord.

If folks see in me any virtue, any goodness, any wisdom, then they see the hand of my Dad. Because of him, I am as good a man as I am. No shortcoming I have can be traced to him or his influence. He was kind, compassionate and helpful to a fault. He was a man of faith and of prayer. He lived the last decade of his life under a form of house arrest imposed by his faulty lungs. But he reached out to others. He was as quick to share his vast knowledge of his sheet metal trade as he was to share his faith in God and his love for family.

Most of you who read this column regularly know, my little granddaughter Caitlyn died in December of 1998. One of my first thoughts as I looked at the earthen vessel that once served the soul of my dad was that Dad was holding Caitlyn—that he had been reunited with our family members who crossed the portal into eternity before him. I am grateful for that thought.

And I am grateful that we had Dad for 30 years after his condition began to sap his life away. I am grateful that Dad and I were able to talk with each other Sunday and Monday, and that his mind was clear until shortly before 3 p.m. Wednesday. I am grateful that I could hold his hand as he passed from us.

"For me to live is Christ and to die is gain," Paul wrote. His gain is our loss. Our loss begets our sorrow. Still, for those of us who believe, our sorrow is mingled with faith and confidence— confidence that we will be reunited in a never-ending day in a land without sickness, sorrow and death.

So if in the next few days you see me and offer condolences, my eyes may mist over and a tear or two may slip down my cheek. Please understand that the tears are not for him—they are for me.

Unheralded goodness abounds

Friday afternoon I arrived in Kinston after being gone nearly two weeks. As those of you know who read last week's column, my father died on Thursday, Sept. 14. I had been with my mom and dad since the previous Sunday while he was in the hospital. After Dad's death, we had funeral arrangements to make and execute.

I want to share just a little about the goodness and compassion of people with you. If you watch TV news or pick up most newspapers, what you discover is that people are basically evil and actively do bad things. People kill each other, steal from each other, deceive each other, sue each other, and engage in all kinds of horrible behaviors. If we are not careful, the vision created on TV screens and in newspapers and magazines will become the reality we accept for truth.

Now, some people actually do terrible things. But the key word is "some." "A few" is even closer to the mark. The nature of the news business is to present the exceptions—not the rules. "Dog bites man" is not news, but "man bites dog" is news, the old editors used to tell us.

My experience teaches me a different truth about people, and this truth was reinforced when my father died. My family received a three-state salute to compassion and goodness. My parents moved to Ohio in 1966 and have lived there since. As soon as the news of Dad's death went out, their friends and neighbors in Ohio went into action. The phone rang constantly. Friends brought food to the house. Cotner's Funeral Home in Reynoldsburg took care of Dad's final needs and arranged to have his body returned to Vinton, Virginia, his hometown. This outpouring of support took place within a few hours of his death.

Then on Friday we traveled to Vinton. By the time we arrived there, another outpouring of support was already underway. Dad has two sisters in Vinton, and most of my cousins live there as well. We stayed with Ricki and Ross, my cousin and her husband. The counters in her kitchen were lined with food brought by neighbors and friends. Over the next three days, three churches furnished us so much food that we considered finding a homeless shelter to take part of it. Now, to help you understand just how much food we received, please keep in mind that our family members alone totaled close to 40 people. We fed family and every well wisher we could persuade to eat.

Dozens of flower arrangements, plants and rock gardens made Lotz Funeral Home in Vinton seem in late spring bloom. Flowers came from friends in North Carolina and from friends in Ohio, from friends in Florida and New York, and from friends in Virginia. My dad was a retired sheet metal worker and a union man. Sheet Metal Local #24 sent a beautiful arrangement in his honor.

I wondered how many folks would be at the visitation Sunday evening. After all, Dad hadn't lived in the Vinton-Roanoke area for 43 years. Whatever misgivings I had were allayed at 6 p.m. when people packed Parlor B of the funeral home. Dad's first cousins and boyhood friends streamed in. They each took a couple of minutes to share a memory of Dad with John and me. Some even gave us pictures of Dad as a boy. Men Dad had worked with stopped in. Some who paid respects were folks who once worked as apprentices under Dad. The visitation, scheduled to last until 8 p.m., went on until close to 8:30.

Mom and I returned to Ohio on Tuesday. She had put a stop on her mail before we left, so Wednesday we drove to the post office to pick up the mail. At least three dozen sympathy cards awaited her. Then I came home to North Carolina Friday to find several plants and at least two dozen cards from friends in this area.

Hundreds and hundreds of people reached out to our family. They fixed food, sent flowers, and offered support and sympathy. Not a single one of them had to do anything. What these people did came from the goodness of their hearts.

And that goodness is what we lose in the face of constant

media bombardments of exception upon exception, of evil upon evil. So the next time you start feeling that people are evil and hopeless villains, look at the obituary page and understand that behind each of those names are dozens, even hundreds, of good people pouring out their support for bereaved families. You might just add a little perspective to the media blitz.

Losing my second Mama

One Sunday in late 1971, I sat at the table in Sandra's home. Joe and Leneave sat with me as Sandra and her mother, Mrs. Dawson, scurried around the kitchen making last minute preparations for Sunday dinner.

I looked on in awe, wondering how Mrs. Dawson planned to get anything else on the huge round table. Fried chicken, ham, creamed potatoes, field peas, green beans, yams, half an onion, homemade biscuits, and butter provided a feast for my eyes and a symphony of aromas for my nose. On that Sunday, Mrs. Dawson introduced me to Southern cooking, Rebie-style.

The food was wonderful. The people were crazy. Joe was an East Carolina student, and Leneave was still a high school student at North Lenoir. Leneave spoke in one of the thickest combinations of country-Southern I'd ever heard. He and Joe did a rapid-fire comedy routine. When Sandra and her mom finally placed the last two dishes and freshened everyone's glass of that powerful concoction Mrs. Dawson called "iced tea," the meal began.

Joe and Leneave had, up to that time, seemed intent on entertaining me, but now they switched strategies. For most of the meal they tried to mildly annoy their mom and embarrass Sandra.

"Hey, Sandra," Leneave said offering a piece of chicken stuck on the end of a fork. "Do ya like t' neck?" Sandra turned crimson, and Mrs. Dawson chided Leneave about his lack of manners. Leneave put on his innocent mask, complete with a hurt expression that his graciousness could be so misunderstood.

A little while later, something akin to a sonic boom went off inside the house.

"Joe Burrell!"

Mrs. Dawson's reprimand nearly covered Joe's "excuse me" and Leneave's raucous outburst of laughter. I have never known any other person who has turned burping into the auditory art Joe displays.

Now, admittedly, my own family could do some strange things during mealtime. Once John asked my dad if he could return thanks before a meal. Dad usually served as the grace-giver, but Dad was so pleased that John asked, he never expected John to have an ulterior motive. By the time John uttered "Amen," his fork was already stuck in a plump pheasant breast from one of the birds he had taken during his latest hunt.

Still, my family's mealtime antics were a county fair compared to the three-ring circus that unfolded before my eyes on that Sunday. What a strange way to try to impress a new beau, I thought. Frankly, they weren't trying to impress me. Joe, Leneave, and Mama engaged in mealtime madness because they so enjoyed being in each other's presence. Theirs was love on the lunatic fringe. If I wanted to marry into this family, I'd have to deal with the insanity—perhaps even enter into it.

The strange thing was that not too much time had to pass once Sandra and I married before calling Mrs. Dawson "Mama" no longer seemed strange. I counted myself fortunate. I had two Mamas—one that birthed me, who lived in Ohio, and one that bore my wife here in North Carolina.

Now, I am down to one Mama again.

Mama Dawson passed away Saturday morning. She had been a patient at Britthaven Nursing Home in Snow Hill when her medical needs finally outstripped our abilities to care for her at home.

But the memories we have of her live just as vividly now as she did when she created them. After knowing her and loving her for almost 30 years, I can tell you she was a wonderful woman of the old school. She had been a farmer's wife, and the survival arts lived strong in her for the years I knew her. She could make a dress, cook, garden, can, and freeze. She had a strong work ethic and worked hard until her body just could no longer perform what her mind knew needed to be done.

Through the years, I came to love and admire her.

I know she loved me, too. She accepted me as part of her family—as one of her sons. She was willing to extend her mother's heart outside the ring of those children she bore and include the spouses her children loved.

Those bonds count deeply when two families become one. They are the bonds that nourish and nurture. They are the bonds that help define true family.

Granny holds special spot

Lady Belle Cundiff was born Feb. 22, 1909. Later she married Henry Solly Parker and took his last name for her own. I can't remember a single piece of mail showing up at her house for Mrs. Lady Belle Parker. As far as I know, she carried—and still carries—his name: Mrs. Henry S. Parker. On Sept. 22, 1928, she took on a new name—mother. And since shortly after Oct. 15, 1950, I have known her simply as "Granny."

Granny's house was always special. As a child I played in her yard. Her yard was huge, a rolling piece of earth that followed the contour of the hill where she lived in the Roanoke Valley of Virginia. We had a swing set on the middle tier of her three-tiered yard. I thrilled at swinging upward, moving closer and closer to the clouds, and then jumping out of the swing at its highest arc, soaring through the air, and thumping down on the bottom tier. How did I manage to survive that fall without a parachute? I always wondered about that.

Granny's house is where I listened to the old Philco radio-record player. At Granny's house, I was first introduced to Tennessee Ernie Ford. I love his singing to this day. On the album Granny and Granddaddy kept in the Philco's cubby,

Tennessee Ernie's rotund bass boomed a spiritual about Noah finding grace in the eyes of the Lord. The song's humor still amuses me.

"Take all these people and creatures to earth. / Don't be more trouble than you're worth," God exhorts Noah in this spiritual version of the story.

I can still hear Jimmie Davis singing "Suppertime" on another album. "Come home. Come home. It's suppertime. The shadows lengthen fast. Come home. Come home; it's suppertime. You're going home at last."

Granny's house was home—a place of perpetual suppertime, a place of yellow cake with chocolate icing, of bacon and eggs and white gravy for breakfast, of fresh-cooked ham and sliced tomatoes and potato salad.

But as I grew up, I realized what made Granny's house so special. Her house is where I could always find Granny, her waist-length hair rolled into a bun and her apron pinned to her dress. A cup of coffee marked her spot at the kitchen table. Since Granny never learned to drive, I never had to worry about showing up and finding her gone. Even if I had shown up and she was not home, I knew I had only to look one house on either side for her—at Mary Ann's or Hester's.

But each time I walked into her house on Cleveland Avenue, she was there. And she was always glad to see me. I was the oldest son of her oldest son—her first grandchild.

"We always thought you were really something," she told me when I visited her on April 24 on my way home to North Carolina. But she was wrong. I am just one of a number of her grandchildren. She is our one and only Granny.

Sandra and I spent our honeymoon at Granny's house. The first time my mom and dad saw Sara, our oldest daughter, they drove from Ohio to meet us at Granny's. I still remember Dad driving all night, coming into the house just when Sara's bottle was just right, snatching the baby from Sandra's arms—and feeding his little granddaughter. Four generations meeting at Granny's. Dad's first grandchild. Granny's first great-grandchild.

I do not think I'll ever forget the times Granny sent us money. She knew what a pitiful salary I made teaching in the Christian school where I worked. Sometimes, we'd open a card, and enclosed was a cardboard kitten, a device filled with the dimes she scrimped and scraped. Sometimes we'd open a letter and a five—or ten-dollar bill would tumble out. We looked on whatever she sent as holy money. We knew how little she had herself.

Granny lived alone for years, maintaining her own home, paying her own way with the pittance she received from Social Security—living with quiet dignity. As she grew older, she needed some help. Uncle Bobby and Aunt Dot live with her now. They take real good care of her, Granny tells me. I'm glad for the care and company Dot and Bobby give to her.

When I stopped by in April, she welcomed me, as she always does.

"Son, it's good to see you," she said, patting my hand. The love I feel for her that sometimes gets pushed to the back by the rush of daily living came flooding to the front, and I looked at her and rejoiced in what she means to me. We talked and she asked me to sing something for her. Suddenly, my sparse gray hair seemed to turn brown and full, and my heartbeat quickens a bit for the joy of spending a little time with her.

Granny, we always thought you were really something.

And you are.

Happy Mother's Day.

CHAPTER SIX

SPECIAL PEOPLE

Real heroes often unseen

When most of us hear the word "hero," we think of a member of the U.S. military charging a machine gun nest, a firefighter saving a child from a blazing building, or an airline pilot who safely lands an ailing aircraft. But most heroes don't fit these descriptions. They perform their heroism in silence, never imagining that they are doing anything out of the ordinary. One of my friends is an example of this silent type of hero. I will not use her name because doing so would offend her modesty. But her example is both noteworthy and symbolic of hundreds of other unsung heroes. Her story needs telling.

A number of months ago her husband began to have a series of strokes. His first stroke appeared minor, giving him only a slight irregularity of speech. His next stroke was not as kind. While stroke after stroke sapped his vitality, a heart attack and a bout with lung cancer complicated his struggle. He was in and out of the hospital. When he was in the hospital, she rarely left his side. She might leave for just a couple of hours a day so she could shower and eat. When a friend was able to sit with her husband during the day, she worked in her beauty shop. After all, the bills still came.

She could be demanding, especially on health professionals.

She learned what expectations she should have for the medical treatment her husband was receiving. She became a watchdog, his advocate. She provided a great deal of his care herself. She never asked anyone to give more than she did or do more than she was willing to do.

When he could no longer feed himself, she fed him. When he became incontinent, she kept him clean. She knew what foods he loved and made sure she always had a supply. I have seen her sit at his side, feeding him, chatting constantly, asking him questions—constantly seeking to challenge his mind in the hopes that he would regain as much normalcy as he could.

When his doctor sent him home, she cared for him there. A friend would sit with him while she worked in the shop within her home. As his condition declined, she refused to take appointments. She told her customers to call. When he was having a good day, she served her customers. When he needed her, she served him.

She always treated him with dignity, respect, compassion and love. When an ailing person seems out of touch with reality, most of us have trouble remembering that a mind—and person—is trapped inside that body. I have seen people talk about such a person in that condition as if the person were not even present. I am afraid I have been guilty of that behavior myself.

But she constantly professed her love to him. She maintained a cheery disposition as she chatted—and hoped— and met his needs. She never talked about him in his presence. She always talked to him and with him. I watched her love him and care for him until his body finally surrendered. I recalled the Bible verse that says God does not put more upon us than we are able to bear. I could not but help to marvel at the stress she graciously endured and the pressures she lovingly bore.

Her faith is strong, although she would never make that claim. As she persevered in her service to him, I gained new insights into the height and depth and breadth and width of her love for him and her faith in God.

I know that she is not the only one who has borne such toil, stress and pressure with grace and dignity. I celebrate her as a sterling example of the unsung heroes who give of themselves and do what they do because they are fulfilling the duties that love and faith demand.

America from the outside

The telephone rang, and when I answered it, I heard a voice from my past.

"Hello, Mike? This is Beth. I think I may be lost a little."

Beth Newton was on her way to my home. For the first time in nearly 20 years, I was going to see her. Our friendship dates back more than 30 years when we were both high school students. Although we did not attend the same school, we went to the same church. After graduation, I wound up at Ohio State and went into teaching. She attended Wheaton College for a year and then studied nursing at Case Western Reserve in Cleveland.

Since then, I had moved to North Carolina and she had dedicated her life to helping the people of rural Haiti. For more than 20 years, she has tended to the health needs of the Haitians and ministered to their spiritual needs, as well. Our church is one of her supporting churches and she was in town to give us an update on her work there.

What impresses her the most when she returns from the four-year terms in Haiti?

"The choices in this country. You have so many things to choose from," she told me as we chatted in my living room. She pointed to the variety of fast food restaurants, the abundance of foods in the supermarkets, and even the different cars we can choose to drive.

We decided that evening to go for pizza at Michael's suggestion. My son Michael thinks pizza is its own food group. Beth was excited.

"Do you get to eat pizza in Haiti?" he asked.

"Oh, yes. We have a lady who cooks for us, and sometimes

when she fixes loaves of bread, she presses some in a flat pan and we make our own." Well, I thought, that's not exactly what I had in mind. "Sometimes getting cheese or pepperoni is not all that easy, but we make out," she added.

As part of her display Beth carries a special doorstop or heavy-duty paperweight. A tarantula was crossing her living room one day in Haiti, so she took a bowl and put it on top of the creature. She slid a plate beneath it and put the makeshift trap in the freezer. Then she turned the frozen spider remains into a doorstop.

Through the clear acrylic, six to eight inches across the top, I could see the huge, hairy tarantula frozen in time. And I thought the North Carolina wolf spiders are big.

When I asked her about her email address, she patiently explained that the part of Haiti she works does not have regular electricity.

"The power comes on at the strangest times," she said, "usually sometime after midnight." One morning she woke early, before 4 a.m., and decided to make a cake. Just as she finished the batter, she heard the whine of the power shutting off. Life in Haiti, she said.

Beth's reports about the people she ministers to in the hospital and clinic touched me most. She mentioned two specific cases. Both of these sick Haitians had AIDS. Nearly 25 percent of the Haitian population is HIV-positive, she said. She extends help to the sick and compassion to the dying. She also offers the gospel of Christ. She doesn't preach. Listening to the gospel is not part of the payment a patient must give to obtain services at the clinic or hospital. She simply mentions her faith, and if the listener responds, she continues, explaining how the listener can have eternal life in Christ.

In a couple of months Beth will be heading back to Haiti, a nation renowned for its poverty. She will take up the life she has come to love, a life of service to body and soul. I could tell that although she has enjoyed her furlough to her homeland, she yearns to be back with those who so desperately need her skill as a nurse practitioner, the light of her smile, and the gospel she lives by.

Who says her hand a needle better fit?

Anyone approaching the front door of Nell Eutsler's home immediately confronts one of her scholarly interests—a brass door knocker shaped like a whale, a tribute to Herman Melville's masterpiece, "Moby-Dick." Drawings and paintings from "Moby-Dick" adorn the walls of her den. Photographs of places she visited during her travels complete the collage.

I visited Nell last week, not at home, but at Lenoir Memorial Hospital.

"I am not afraid to die, but I'm going to be mad as hell if I do," she told me when I entered her room. "I've got so many things I want to finish."

She needed to proof the galleys of an article concerning Robert Herrick's epigrams scheduled to appear in the Mount Olive Review. She had just received a copy of her entry in the Dictionary of Literary Biography on Sir John Fortescue, a 15th-century British legal thinker who wrote a book that Nell believed was one of the forerunners of modern children's literature. She wanted to revise the entry before its publication. She wanted to redo two of her earlier papers, one on poet Walt Whitman and another on theologian Paul Tillich. She had been toying with a major revision of her thesis on Melville's "Encantadas." Nell was working on all these projects after retiring as professor emeritus from East Carolina University's English faculty in 1983.

Her projects remain unfinished. At 4:30 a.m., Thursday, Oct. 7, Nell died.

I know she is mad as hell—not because she died, but because she did not have time to finish all the things her active mind struggled to complete.

I moved to Kinston in 1971, and I lived here for a few years before I met Nell, but I can't recall a time I did not know her. Because of her, I met people I wouldn't have met otherwise. One night we traveled to East Carolina to hear noted inventor and thinker Buckminster Fuller. Bucky, as she called him, was spending the night at her home after the lecture because he was flying out of Kinston's jetport the next day. I rode with them from Greenville to Kinston, privileged to listen. In Nell's den I met Jackie Torrance, one of this nation's premiere storytellers.

Nell corresponded regularly with Native American writer Jamake Highwater. She shared that correspondence with me. Nell and I worked together for several years on A Carolina Literary Companion, a literary journal once published by Kinston's Community Council for the Arts.

What I will miss most about her are our working lunches. Lunch with Nell was always an intellectual experience—a discussion period, a time spent examining ideas or analyzing the relative merits of short stories for the journal.

I never had to wonder who was on the phone when Nell called. Her voice was distinctive. I never had to wonder what she thought about any subject or issue we discussed. She always offered cogent presentations of her ideas.

She sprang from pioneer stock. Her mother crossed the Kansas prairie in a wagon as a child, and the family took up residence near White Water. Nell retained that pioneer spirit in her intellectual inquiry. Although she traveled to Russia, China, India, Australia, Germany, and South America, the longest journeys she took were pilgrimages of the mind and soul.

I will miss sharing those journeys.

Retired judge served the people well

Many of you remember a young man who cut his judicial teeth as a district court judge only to move up to the superior court bench. His name is Paul Wright. The recent scramble to appoint a new district attorney and superior court judge stem from Paul's decision to retire from the judgeship he held since 1984. For more than 20 years, Paul served the people of Wayne, Greene and Lenoir counties—as well as the people of this state.

We all have our notions of what the courtroom is like. Too many of us think that court is a cross between "L.A. Law" and "The People's Court." Paul gave me a different view of the judiciary. Since he is a close personal friend, I took time to watch him in action in the courtroom. When he started as a district court judge, he often processed 125 cases a day in the courts of our three counties. Traffic tickets, child support judgments, criminal cases, show cause orders, civil court, juvenile court. The volume of cases that passed through his courtroom each day reminded me of Raleigh at rush hour.

Yet the people I knew who had stood before Judge Wright—either as victim or victimizer—praised him for his fairness and common sense. They sensed—even when they lost a case—that Paul had listened to the facts and rendered an honest decision. The confidence area people had in Paul's quality as a judge demonstrated itself in his first superior court race. Paul was seeking to unseat an incumbent superior court judge in 1984, and the people of Lenoir and Greene counties gave him nearly 70 percent of their votes. Because of that support, Paul became the first person to defeat a sitting North Carolina superior court judge since the 1950s—no small achievement for a man who was 36 years old and offered only six years of experience as a judge.

Being a superior court judge is grueling work. I watched Paul in action one day and remember one lawyer objecting to a question his counterpart posed to a witness. Paul stopped, placed his fingers in the form of a steeple, rested his nose on the steeple, and pondered. After a pause of nearly a minute, he overruled the objection. The questioning continued. I once caught a glimpse of his notes and understood that he listened more meticulously to testimony than did the jurors hearing the case.

Just a couple of months ago, some of Paul's friends invited me to his 50th birthday party. In fact, they asked me to Emcee the event. Those attending represented a cross-section of Paul's various interests and friendships. Some old Goldsboro friends and political allies took time to attend. Church friends were present. Even his secretary and her husband were there.

I decided Paul needed a little roasting, so far the dinner, I started it off. We took turns giving him a few friendly gibes and gag gifts. Someone gave him pads and pens—a token of how he talks and draws at the same time. Another gave Paul something akin to a "Dick Tracy" watch. We agreed that if Paul could have only added a telephone to his calculator watch, he would have been in paradise. In the end, what emerged from the roasting was a genuine affection and deep respect for him as a man.

For six months at a time, Paul would be assigned to hold court in one of the counties of this state. He spent six months on the Outer Banks. He spent six months in Wilmington. He spent six months in Lenoir County. Such travel was not easy for Paul. Serving in distant counties often took him away from his wife, Lisa, and their small children. Sometimes he rented houses so that his family could be with him. Too many times we forget the human side of those who serve our courts.

Now Paul Wright is a private citizen—a retired private citizen. In some ways, I envy him that freedom. In others, I am glad I did not have to pay the price he did of long hours, tedious work, and incessant travel. I am glad for him, for Lisa, and for his children. But I am sad for our courts because we have lost one of the most respected men of integrity who sat on the judicial bench.

Appearances sometimes mislead

Not long ago I was talking with Richard Parker, who works at Garner Funeral Home. He told me a story that seems worth repeating.

One evening, while Richard was working, a man entered the funeral home. Richard saw the man come in and suspected that he was not a friend or family member of the deceased. For one thing, the man was dirty and unkempt. For another, his clothes were little more than tatters.

"I figured he was just a bum," Richard said. "When he

walked up to me and asked for money, he confirmed my suspicions. He told me he had been out of work and had no home. He asked me to 'lend' him a little money so he could get something to eat." Of course, Richard saw this man as a problem. He did not want this bum's presence upsetting the loved ones of the deceased. Richard wanted to get rid of the man as quickly as possible.

"I reached into my pocket and grabbed all my lose change—no more than a couple of dollars," he said. "I gave the man the money and ushered him outside as quickly as I could. I told him we were busy with visitation and that he needed to leave." When the bum took the money and left, Richard was relieved. A couple of bucks in change was a small price to pay to get rid of a potential problem.

A few days passed and Richard put the incident out of his mind. After all, he had been panhandled before—just like most of us have. You give the panhandler a little money and, hopefully, he goes away and leaves you alone. I have given away my share of loose change before.

"Did you give a guy some money the other night," a coworker asked him.

"Yes I did," Richard replied. "A few days ago a bum came in here with a hard luck story and asked me for some money. I gave him a couple of dollars in change to get rid of him. We were having visitation that night and I didn't want this bum creating a scene."

"Well, the guy stopped by here yesterday and asked me to give you this," the coworker replied. Then he handed Richard two crumpled dollar bills. Richard was stunned. He certainly never expected to see that money again. In fact, he thought two bucks was a cheap price to pay to avoid a scene. As he looked at the two bills, his eyes misted as he suddenly realized he had misjudged the man.

"I felt ashamed of myself," Richard said. "I figured this guy was just a bum, a panhandler, a beggar—maybe even worse. But this guy went out of his way to return the money I had given him. I certainly wasn't looking for the money back. Now I feel bad for judging him so harshly."

What's the big deal about two bucks? I think that's exactly the point. The recipient of Richard's brusque generosity had to know that Richard never expected to see the money again. As far as I know, Richard and the man did not exchange names. Why would someone in obvious need go out of his way to return such a small amount of money? I am sure that two dollars meant much more to this tattered fellow than it does to Richard. Evidently somewhere in this man's code of behavior is the notion that if a person borrows money, then the person is obliged to repay the debt—even if the debt is small.

In a day when panhandlers seem to be on every street corner, we can easily become jaded. We can write off every person who asks for money as some bum just looking for a handout. We usually resent them, shove a little money their way, and hope we can avoid a confrontation or scene. As one song says, "It's easy to be hard."

But not everyone who asks for money is necessarily a bum. Some folks are what my dad calls "down on their luck." What we give them as a handout may really turn out to be a helping hand. Unfortunately, appearance doesn't help us determine who is looking for a handout and who is looking for a hand up. Richard learned that lesson from a man who stopped by one night.

It's alright, Ma,...He's only 60

In early 1968 I slid "John Wesley Harding" from its dust jacket, gently placed it on the turntable, and listened as Bob Dylan intoned the title track about an Old West version of Robin Hood.

"John Welsey Harding was a friend to the poor. / He traveled with a gun in every hand. / All along this countryside he opened many-a door, / But he was never known to hurt an honest man."

About 40 minutes later, I started the record again, pencil in hand, eager to transcribe the lyrics. I listened yet again—over and over—to figure out the chord progressions. I wanted to be able to play and sing all Dylan's new songs.

I was just 17, a high school senior looking forward to graduation and then college. Dylan was already firmly established at Number One in my pantheon of musical deities. A new release was a holy event, a time to savor the word play, the subtle melodies, the raspy voice so many mocked.

I loved the harmonies of Peter, Paul and Mary. Donovan was "mellow-yellowing" before any soft drink bore that name. The Beatles and Rolling Stones churned out hit after hit. Motown added its flavor. However, for me and many others growing up in "The Sixties," Dylan was our voice, our prophet.

This week, the man who reportedly advised young people to distrust anyone over 30 turns twice 30. Imagine: Bob Dylan at 60.

"John Wesley Harding" was Dylan's ninth album. He has recorded 33 others since that time. Does this aging rock icon still have impact on the music scene? Just this year he won the "Best Song" Golden Globe Award and the "Best Song" Oscar for "Things Have Changed," a song in the film "Wonder Boys."

He won Grammys in 1997 for his album "Time Out of Mind." Ever heard of it? Not sure? Well, if you saw the film "Hope Floats," then you heard Garth Brooks sing, "To Make You Feel My Love." That song is one of the cuts from Dylan's "Time Out of Mind." Then again, you may be more familiar with Billy Joel's version of the same song.

Who counts Dylan as a mentor? You'd be surprised just how far-reaching his influence is. According as a USA Today article, Bruce Springsteen said, "Everybody owes [Dylan] a debt." Springsteen and Dylan have performed together. Dylan has also teamed with Tom Petty, Carlos Santana, Paul Simon, G.E. Smith of the old "Saturday Night Live" band, Joan Baez, Willie Nelson, Johnny Cash—the list goes on and on. Dylan advised U2's Bono to get in touch with his roots in Irish folk music. Stephen Stills said Dylan was his inspiration to write. David Bowie honored Dylan with "Song for Bob Dylan."

I can still remember hearing the O'Jays sing their version

of Dylan's "Emotionally Yours." Jimi Hendrix covered Dylan's "All Along the Watchtower." Stevie Wonder did an R&B version of "Blowin' in the Wind." The Byrds recorded "Mister Tambourine Man," and the Turtles produced their version of "It Ain't Me, Babe."

Now, 32 years after I spent hours transcribing the words from "John Wesley Harding," I still hold Dylan in high esteem as songwriter, poet, and visionary. I respect him because he has never sold out to musical whim and pop fads. In fact, Dylan has never seemed quite aligned with conventional music in any period. He's always gone his own way. Even when he was booed at the Newport Folk Festival for going electric. He stayed true to himself even when he was criticized for performing his gospel music from "Slow Train," "Saved," and "Shot of Love" to the neglect of his other songs during what has been called his gospel phase. During his 1986 tour of Australia, he opened his show with a "song about [his] hero"—and then sang, "In the Garden"—a song about the arrest, death and resurrection of Christ.

He has had the courage to—well, be himself. In a world striving to create appearances, Dylan has had the guts to be real and to tell the truth as he saw it. In the process, he has given us some of the best poetry written in the second half of the 20th century—and the beginning of the 21st.

Granddad lost in 'perfect storm'

Although Gloucester, Mass., is the northernmost point of the Intercoastal Waterway, this small fishing village has gotten a little closer than the nearly 800 miles it lies to the north of us. A new movie, "The Perfect Storm," has brought the hard lives of Gloucester fishing men and their families to life on the big screen. Toward the end of the film, the camera's eye pans the list of fishermen who lost their lives to crashing waves, fierce storms, and chilling temperatures. This story, backed by a wall of hundreds of names, reaches our hearts and souls with a sense of tragedy born of determination.

But to one area man "The Perfect Storm" was an unnecessary reminder of the hard living, hard drinking, hard dying men of Gloucester. If you see the film, look for one special name as it flits by: Cavanaugh, James J. This Gloucester fisherman died in 1951 when the Gudrem, a steel-beamed trawler, went down in the icy waters off Gloucester in one of the areas many "perfect storms." James J. Cavanaugh was the grandfather of Jim Cavanaugh, the chaplain at Dobbs School.

Jim, who was born in Gloucester in 1952, said his family did not go to the "Crow's Nest," the tavern featured in the movie. Instead, his family frequented Mitch's Tavern.

"You basically went there, got drunk, and fought," he said. "It was the Gloucester fisherman's form of entertainment." Until 1952, when the state built a bridge to the island, the people of Gloucester were isolated from the "mainlanders." Yet, Jim says, despite its isolation, the small fishing village had a cosmopolitan atmosphere.

"I remember once running into my house and saying, 'Mom, the pirates are here,' because I heard two swarthy men speaking a foreign language." In fact, even today, the island is a mixture of the traditional fishing families who have called Gloucester home for hundreds of years with others who hail from Ireland, Portugal and Italy.

"The village is not really a melting pot—it's more like a stew," Jim explains. He said the Italian contingent holds the "Festival of St. Peter" in the same manner their ancestor's celebrated it in the Old World. When the fleet takes to the waters during the first of the new fishing season, the Cardinal comes from Boston to sprinkle the boats with holy water in a ceremony the islanders call "The Blessing of the Fleet."

The life of a Gloucester fisherman is harsh. They go out to sea for two weeks and "work mind-numbing 12-hours shifts." They "hot bunk," which means that while one man works, the other sleeps. Since the boats do not have enough bunks for all the men, two men share the bunk, so the bunk is always warm.

"If you get back—if you survive—you celebrate. You go to the tavern and get drunk while the lumpers—the people on the dock who pull the fish from the hold and ice and box them—unload the boat."

Each boat has a special flag that flies when someone dies during the trip. Jim said it was common to see those flags flying. As boats approached the harbor, Gloucester families lined the docks to look for those flags.

Jim said that the film showed the boats leaving during bright sunlight, but more often than not, the boats left during a "pea-souper," a fog so thick that the fishermen couldn't even see the bow of the boat. His grandfather knew how to navigate the harbor using nothing but sounds—bells on the buoys or foghorns on the lighthouses.

Jim's grandfather survived two shipwrecks, he said, because the boats went down in the summer. The storm that claimed his grandfather's life was a winter storm. When his grandfather hit the waves, he could not have survived the frigid water more than 30 seconds, a minute at most.

The words of Psalm 107:23-24 grace the base of the statue honoring the lost fishermen of Gloucester. Those words read: "They that go down to the sea in ships, that do business in great waters; These see the works of the LORD, and his wonders in the deep." The message has two keen edges: it reminds people of the wonders of the sea—it warns them of its dangers and death.

Every year the people of Gloucester hold a special ceremony. The whole town gathers along the shore of the cut in Gloucester Harbor and lay flowers in the water as the tide heads out to sea.

"It's our way of remembering them. We can't visit a cemetery, so this is our way of going to the grave."

What is wrong with kids today?

Since Feb. 2, 1996, 37 students or teachers have died at school, their lives snuffed out by 14 different students. Of those totals, 15 include the dead from Columbine High School in

Littleton, Colorado. The Columbine killers took the lives of a teacher, 12 fellow students—and then their own.

What is wrong with kids today? Folks ask me that question all the time. I have no idea why. What's wrong with kids today?

Let me take you to another scene. Time and date: 7 p.m., Thursday, April 29, 1999. Place: King's Restaurant. Occasion: The North Lenoir High School Academic Banquet. Teachers, administrators, parents and special guests gathered to honor the 141 North Lenoir students who maintained an "A" average for the entire academic year. I am not sure just how many students attend North Lenoir, but my guess is somewhere around 1,100—so these 141 represent the top 13 percent of the students.

This same scene was repeated for Kinston High students and South Lenoir High students. Hundreds of students who went to school, worked hard, studied their collective behinds off—who aimed for excellence and attained it.

What is wrong with kids today?

If we are talking about the overwhelming majority of our students, nothing is wrong with them. The fact that hundreds of students were being honored for academic achievement is so common that not a single reporter from the AP, UPI, Reuters, ABC, NBC, CBS, CNN or any other national or state news agency showed up at King's Restaurant to film the unfolding drama.

Instead, hundreds of columns inches of stories and photos, and dozens of news clips and interviews on TV, highlighted the work of the disgusting duo of Littleton. If we are not careful, the media will distort our sense of who our kids really are.

On that Thursday, I sat across from Kelli Kirk, a North Lenoir senior who is not only an outstanding student, but who also works as editor of the yearbook, serves as co-captain of the soccer team, and played on the volleyball team last fall. Kelli will attend the University of North Carolina at Chapel Hill in August.

A couple of rows over sat Daniel Anderson, who last year won second place in the state for bodybuilding. In the fall,

Daniel will head to North Carolina State on scholarship. Across the table from Daniel sat Deric Phillips, already accepted into the honors program at East Carolina and another scholarship recipient.

Jaime Britt and Jonas Howard sang "Something Good" from the North Lenoir production of "The Sound of Music." Jaime will become a part of the Mount Olive singers next year. She competed against 500 other students for the single available spot open in that illustrious group.

Jaime, Daniel, Deric, Kelli—these students and their fellow honorees are much more representative of the next generation heading toward maturity than the two misguided boys who pulled the triggers that ended the lives of 12 of their classmates.

The older students among these honorees not only maintain outstanding grades, but they compete in sports, hold down part-time jobs, and are active in community service and churches. They successfully juggle all these responsibilities— and they excel. Just ask their pastors, their bosses, their teachers, their coaches.

I do not know every student at North Lenoir. I don't even know all of the 141 honored that recent Thursday night. However, based on the students I do know, our future is not only secure—but it is bright.

Young folks, as you listen to all the doomsayers belittle your generation, please remember that one old Baby Boomer believes in you—and thanks God for you.

Thanks to all our rescuers

Down East has been inundated with two floods since Hurricane Floyd tore through our part of North Carolina and dumped a foot or two of rain on us.

When we hear the word flood, we obviously think of the waters that traveled beyond what most disaster forecasters called our 500-year flood plain. These waters buried cars, submerged buildings, inundated farms, drowned livestock, drenched crops, covered roads, undermined bridges, swamped water treatment facilities...but you've seen the same footage I've seen, so you know.

But another flood is just as obvious. We have experienced a flood of rescuers who brought their time, energies, bodies and goodwill to our aid. Now, I would not presume to try thanking everyone and every organization by name because I just don't know all their names. I want them to know I am grateful for their hard work and encouragement. I am sure I speak for the vast majority of Down East families.

Carolina Power and Light arranged to have a half million workers on the scene after Hurricane Floyd left this state. These workers came from Ohio, Virginia and Alabama—and probably other states—to restore lights and power to our communities.

Just a couple of days ago at Smith's Cafe I met some folks from Alabama. They work for a tree removal company in the home of the Crimson Tide. Just after the hurricane moved north of us, these Alabama folks began their trek northeastward—and many ended up right here in Kinston and Lenoir County.

"How many of you folks made the trip?" I asked one of the workers.

"Well, at first our company sent 175 men. Now, there's about 35 of us left," he replied.

In Wal-mart I ran into two National Guard personnel from Charlotte. I was behind them at the checkout. When one of them looked back, I caught his eye.

"I just want to thank you folks for everything you are doing for us."

"No problem," he said. He told me he remembered when Hugo went through Charlotte. He recalled the help that poured into Charlotte. "We had a lot of trees down, but this flooding is really something."

"Worse than the flooding we had after Hurricane Fran," I replied. "How much longer you guys going to be here?"

"We're not sure, but we know we'll be here at least two more weeks from today," he said. "But we'll stay as long as you folks need us."

I left Wal-mart to stop by Food Lion for a few groceries. As I walked toward the store, a woman passed by and told me it was closed. I turned toward my car when I heard someone ask if I had jumper cables. The man asking was a civilian standing near a National Guard truck.

"Sure do," I replied. I broke out my heavy-duty cables.

"We are in luck," a National Guardsman called to his friends. While the man connected the cables, I asked the guardsmen where they were from.

"Mount Airy," one said.

"You guys are a good ways from home. Mount Airy is about five hours from here," I said.

"Yeah, but it took us 11 hours to get here. The roads were so bad in places that we had to backtrack."

By now the truck was running.

"Do you know how to get to the Winn Dixie from here?" the guardsman asked.

"Sure do," I said, starting to outline the path. Then I thought of the traffic and the roadblocks. "Are you sure the Winn Dixie will be open?"

"Yeah, it was open last night after all the other stores were closed," he said.

"I'll tell you what," I said. "I need some things, too. How about if I lead you there?"

In a few minutes we were on the way, winding along the back roads, north up US 258, then south down Hull Road, left on Rouse Road...and finally to the Winn Dixie.

"Thank you," the guys called as they crossed the parking lot toward the store.

"No...thank you," I called back.

'Big C' meets bigger 'C'

Kinston High School's football field looked like Camelot readied for a jousting tournament as Lenoir County's 2001 Relay for Life kicked off Friday evening. Tents crowded together and more than 1,000 people gathered for the opening exercises. But the participants did not come to prove themselves on the field of battle. They gathered to unify efforts against a common foe—cancer in all its insidious forms.

Cancer. The Big C. Webster's New World College Dictionary even lists "Big C" as an entry.

About 200 cancer survivors attended the opening exercises. Each stepped briefly to the microphone to give his or her name and the length of survival. Many told where cancer struck their bodies. Some gave brief thanks and tributes.

The cumulative effect of their words left several clear messages: they have hope, they are grateful—and they are courageous. In these survivors, the "Big C" meets a bigger "C"—courage. I've seen that courage as close as I can without suffering from the disease myself.

In 1998, Sandra spent the bulk of the year enduring one treatment for cancer after another. Her courage made me stand in awe. Her courage to go through the chemotherapy. The cycle lasted three weeks. Chemo, sickness, feeling better, feeling nearly normal—then chemo again. Her courage to go through surgery. Her courage to endure high dose chemotherapy with stem cell replacement. Her courage to face radiation treatments day after day until she completed all 33.

She showed her courage in the way she dealt with the fatigue, the way she kept going when she didn't really feel like going. She had courage to eat when she didn't feel like eating. She demonstrated courage and compassion as she dealt with the insensitivity of some who have never had to face anything remotely similar to cancer.

She had the courage to live—and to go on living.

Some of the survivors thanked the Lord—and Sandra and I certainly relate to those sentiments. Some of the survivors thanked the medical staff of the Cancer Center here in Kinston. We understand those feelings. Rarely a day goes by now that Sandra and I do not remember the kindness and hard work of the staff at the Leo Jenkins Center in Greenville.

People I knew stepped to the mike to share their length

of survival—and I hadn't even known some of them had had cancer. So many who fight this battle keep their struggle quiet.

Some people were surprised I wore my sunglasses Friday evening. Yes, the sun was bright when we first arrived, but I knew I would need them for another reason—to conceal tears. Once the survivors finished sharing, they took their victory lap. The rest of us stood around the track, cheered our hearts out, and dabbed our eyes. I blotted at my eyes behind the sunglasses.

I want to thank this community for its dedication to eradicating cancer in all its forms. Our county's Relay for Life is one of the most successful in the entire nation. Last year's event raised $184,000 for cancer research. This year's relay is sure to top that total. Each dollar raised here in Lenoir County is worth three dollars by the time it becomes cancer research funds at East Carolina, at UNC-Chapel Hill, at Duke, and at Bowman-Gray. Our state is at the forefront of the battle against cancer—and our county helps lead the way to fund that research.

To those of you who organized this event, who participated as team members, who raised money and gave your time and effort to make our Relay for Life one of the nation's best, I pray God's richest blessings for you.

Managing editor made a difference

Dear Tom:

I knew sooner or later this day would come. But that knowledge did not make Saturday any easier for me and for the others on this staff who came to know, respect and care for you.

For the past seven years, we have been friends, co-workers and nearly brothers. I remember when you first showed up at the paper, an eager 25-year-old who had taken a job as a sports writer to escape the harsh demands of radio advertising sales. Sports was not your favorite beat. You were always better at shooting photos of sporting events than writing about them. I never really understood how an ex-high school athlete and

Carolina grad could care so little about sports.

You escaped again when the paper needed a court reporter. Covering the courts was red beef and beer to you. You thrived. You made the beat yours. You were good at turning the complexities of legal cases into something a Free Press reader could understand.

You served this paper well.

Then you became news editor. Remember how Mike Kohler planned to groom you for an editor's job? In no time, Mike took a job with First Financial and you ended up managing the newsroom. You knew you were not ready for that responsibility. Still, you did your best to do the job, learning all you could, becoming better every day. I like to think I helped a little as you fought the challenges—and won.

We shared a special bond then and now.

I saw you grow from hesitancy into certainty, from embattled leader to king of the mountain. You took a paper in serious need of innovation and made it better. You have built a solid news staff, and their loyalty to you reflects just how close a bond exists between you and them.

I believe you became as good as you could be here. Now is time for you to move on. You have met the challenges here. New challenges await you in Greensboro. You are blessed with tenacity and a healthy ego—both essential qualities in the newspaper business.

Despite your experiences in Chapel Hill and those to come in Greensboro, your roots are sunk deep in eastern North Carolina soil. The things you have learned and lived here are the things that shape who and what you are. Blossom where you are, but draw your nourishment and strength from your native soil.

Remember us when you edit a story and someone has forgotten that teenager has a hyphen in AP style. Remember us when you read a story about government taking advantage of an executive session to do its dirty business. Some of your proudest battles were against closed-door government in Lenoir County. Remember us when you hear laughter in the newsroom, even if that laughter is your own.

Our best wishes and hopes for your future go with you.
Your friend,
Mike

❧

What kind of young people?

Sandra and I decided to make a whirlwind trip of Ohio to visit my parents over the Fourth of July holiday weekend. One of our prime purposes was to introduce Haley, our newest granddaughter, to her great-grandparents. On the way to Reynoldsburg, Ohio, we spent the night in Mount Airy to break the trip into two easier pieces.

I am usually an early riser. If I had a favorite flower, it would be the morning glory. I wake up—and get up. To say that Sandra is not an early riser is like saying that Niagara Falls leaks a little water. Haley likes to sleep even later than her Grandma. Of course, Haley is only four months old.

So when I woke Saturday, I decided to read a newspaper as I grabbed a little continental breakfast. The lead story of the Mount Airy News told of two local teens accused of murdering 58-year-old Henry Gallant last Sunday. The prosecutor will seek the death penalty for Jacob Robertson and Danny Hazelwood, the two young men who allegedly beat Gallant to death. Both teens have criminal records.

As I thumbed through the newspaper, I noticed that the local editorial focused on this brutal murder. I could feel the editor's outrage as I read. The editor noted that Hazelwood was "grinning and joking around with several other youths as if they all were headed to summer camp."

Then the editor posed this question: "Where has this nation gone wrong in raising a generation of young people who apparently are so callous toward human life—killing and laughing about the situation?" Frankly, I took offense at that assertion. I have a 19-year-old son. He certainly does not fit the portrait of "young people" this editor sketched.

But just how unjust that portrait is came home even more forcefully a little later in the day. We took an exit in West Virginia to give Haley a chance to escape the car seat and stretch a little. To be honest, Grandma and Grandpa needed a stretch, too. As we sat in a Burger King just off Interstate 77, a host of teens suddenly invaded the Home of the Whopper. They wore tee shirts that identified them as members of United Methodist churches in the Cleveland, Ohio area. The backs of their shirts bore the image of a surfer who had "North Carolina" emblazoned on his surfboard.

Now, for those of you who may not remember, a four-month-old baby is a magnet to teens, and soon several of these young people surrounded our table to get a look at Haley as they waited their turn in line. I told them we were from North Carolina.

"Really," one girl said. "We're just coming back from North Carolina."

"Yes," another added. "We were down in the Burgaw area helping rebuild homes of people who were flooded out after the hurricane."

"We had no idea how devastating the flooding was down there," said still another. "They showed us the water marks on people's houses and on stores. I just couldn't believe how much these people suffered and how much they lost."

"Did you get any flooding where you live?" the first one asked.

I told them of the devastation we suffered here in Kinston. How hundreds lost their homes. How flood debris lined roadsides for months as people tried to salvage what little they could of their previous lives. These young folks listened. They expressed genuine concern. They had put their compassion into action.

I asked how many of them had made the trip to North Carolina.

"More than 100," one of the teens said. One hundred young people from four churches. When I returned home, I found a news story in our paper about the efforts of scores of other young people in our own area. They came here as part of

Christian Endeavor.

I thought back to the question the Mount Airy editor had raised: "Where has this nation gone wrong in raising a generation of young people who apparently are so callous toward human life—killing and laughing about the situation?"

If guilty of murder, Hazelwood and Robertson certainly represent the worst of our young people. But these two are the lunatic exception, not the rule. Hazelwood and Robertson do not represent the genuine character of our young people today. These hundreds of nameless kids who gave up a week or two to travel hundreds of miles to assist people they don't even know—they are truer representatives of today's teens.

I wish the Mount Airy editor had met some of these kids. The editor would have a more hopeful perspective on Generation X.

CHAPTER SEVEN

AMERICAN PRIDE

'Old Glory' still inspires

I am nearly ashamed to admit this fact, but when my wife Sandra and I made a recent trip to the Smithsonian in Washington, DC, that trip marked my first—or maybe second—visit ever to our nation's museum row. I may have visited the Smithsonian when I was 11 or 12 on a school trip, but don't remember. I do remember riding the train from Richmond to Washington, and I also remember visiting Mount Vernon. However, no clear recollections of the Smithsonian seem etched in my mind.

Since today is Memorial Day, a holiday first celebrated on May 30, 1868, I thought I'd share one of the most impressive sights I saw at the Smithsonian's National Museum of American History. Frankly, I saw a number of impressive sights. When we emerged from the Metro station, we were standing on the Mall in Washington. Our Capitol Building stands at one end. The Washington Monument soared to my left. A few blocks later, led by our guides, daughter Lydia and her beau R.C., Sandra and I stood outside the museum.

We entered the museum, and once our eyes adjusted to the dimmer light inside, we saw we were facing an enormous flag. I immediately crossed the lobby to get a closer look. I did not need to get closer to see the flag—if that flag had been flying outside, I could have seen it from anywhere on the Mall. What I wanted to see was the historical information at the flag's base.

I was gazing on "The Star-Spangled Banner." No, the flag was not a replica. This flag was the same flag that had flown over Fort McHenry during the War of 1812 when our nation struggled to keep its independence from Great Britain.

This very flag flew the night Francis Scott Key waited as a British naval assault battered Fort McHenry. British ships fired 190-pound exploding shells into the fort for hours, trying to bash it into surrender. American gunners inside fired so few times that the British leaders thought the Americans had given up. British ships, like wolves moving in for the kill, came into the range of Fort McHenry's guns. Maj. George Armistead, commander of Fort McHenry, leapt to the parapets as three of the British ships closed. Then Armistead gave the order to fire. The Americans unleashed a barrage of fire that drove the British back and let them know the Yanks still had plenty of fight left.

Key was being detained on a truce ship in the harbor. He spent a fitful night wondering if the fort would hold. Just before dawn he saw "Old Glory" waving defiantly and knew the Americans had held. Moved by the sight, Key took his pen and wrote the words that we hear sung at nearly every athletic contest: "Oh, say, can you see, by the dawn's early light, what so proudly we hailed at the twilight's last gleaming...."

"The Star-Spangled Banner" was huge in its original form: 30 feet high and 42 feet long. Time has taken its toll, and now the flag is 30 by 34. Even a casual observer must notice how different it is from our flag today. Instead of the familiar 50 stars, this flag has only 15. But instead of 13 stripes, the Fort McHenry banner has 15. Early in our nation's history, Congress added a new star and a new stripe to the flag each time a new state joined the union. Original cost of this hand-made national icon? I saw the receipt: $574.44. It was created in July and August of 1813.

By the way, the original title of the poem Key wrote was not "The Star-Spangled Banner." Key called the poem

"The Defense of Fort McHenry." Soon after that, the name changed—and people began to sing the poem set to a popular pub song brought to America from England. The words and music became the national anthem in 1931—more than 100 years after this nation's people were already singing the song.

In 1907, Key's grandson donated the flag, faded by weather and age, to the Smithsonian. His generosity turned a family treasure into a national one.

Remembering freedom's cost

As you drive down Queen Street the next few weeks, you will notice 50 U.S. flags flying courtesy of the Woodsmen of the World and Pride of Kinston. Terah Archie told me the flags would fly from now until July 4.

Those flags fly in tribute to those who paid with their blood and bodies the awful cost of our freedom. They fly in honor of those who did not share the street-smart notion that teaches us to preserve self at all costs. They fly in respect for those who believed fighting, killing and dying are sometimes the price our nation must pay for a more secure tomorrow.

Today is Memorial Day, a day we honor the brave men and women who died fighting our wars. The holiday was originally called Decoration Day because Americans of the past traditionally marked the day by parades, memorial speeches and ceremonies, and the decoration of graves with flowers and flags.

Memorial Day was first observed on May 30, 1868, on the order of General John Alexander Logan for the purpose of decorating the graves of the American Civil War dead. The day of tribute was observed on May 30 until 1971, when most states changed to a newly established federal schedule of holiday observance.

What are your plans for today? Flying any flags? Spending any time sharing personal, family and national history about those who crawled through the mud, stormed hills and trenches, or felt the quake of falling bombs and mortar shells?

During the Revolutionary War 4,435 men gave their lives in combat to win independence from Great Britain. Another 2,260 died fighting during the War of 1812. When we fought against Mexico, 1,733 were killed in combat.

Then we arrived at the American cataclysm, the Civil War. During that war, we managed to kill 184,594 of each other on the battlefields. (Another 373,458 died of the deprivations of war, from diseases, through accidents, and as prisoners of war.) The Spanish-American War claimed 385 combat dead. Only the Gulf War of 1992 claimed fewer—148 combat dead.

Of course, the World Wars demanded their blood sacrifices. During World War I 53,513 died on the battlefield, and the United States sacrificed 292,131 to World War II. U.S. combat dead from Korea numbered 33,651, and the Vietnam battlefield toll was 47,369. Total combat deaths for these 10 conflicts: 620,219 if my math is correct—620,219 men and women killed in actual combat. Add to that figure another 576,393 service personnel who died during the war but not directly on the battlefield.

Those figures bring the total to nearly 1.2 million dead.

I think of Uncle Jake, my mom's half-brother. He was one of those who stormed the beaches during the Normandy Invasion and lived. In all the time I knew him, he never talked about the experience. If anyone asked about D-Day, he turned pale and shook. He was part of the vast majority of the 16.3 million soldiers, sailors, and Marines we sent to fight World War II who came home. He saw the price of resisting tyranny first hand. He saw—and remembered—and trembled.

We do precious little remembering on Memorial Day. This day seems a memorial to just how little respect we show to the memory of the 1.2 million Americans who gave their lives for our nation, state, counties, communities.

They deserve better.

And so do their comrades in arms who returned home from these bloody conflicts.

As you drive down Queen Street, look at those flags snapping in the breeze and thank the Lord for those who gave their all. Remember this: Each of those flags represents 24,000 Americans who died so we could live free.

Beauty of the Electoral College

I wanted to write this before the final presidential election results are in so no one can accuse me of favoring of George W. Bush or Al Gore. Right now, given the muddle in Florida, either candidate could take that state's 25 electoral votes and win the election. This election, more than any other in recent history, shows that the Electoral College is a wonderful institution created to maintain balance among the varied interests in this country.

I guess by now you have heard—dozens of times—that the people do not directly elect the President of the United States. The U.S. presidency is not decided by a popularity contest. Instead, when you voted on Tuesday, Nov. 7, you actually voted for a slate of electors who will meet Dec. 18 to cast their ballots for president.

Most states have a winner-take-all rule for electors. In short, the candidate that wins the popular vote in a state wins all that state's electoral votes—the total of the number of members a state has in the U.S. House of Representatives, plus two for its Senators. North Carolina has 12 representatives and two senators, so this state has 14 electoral votes. Two states, Maine and Nebraska, are not winner-take-all states.

Now, contrary to popular belief, the United States is not a democracy—and was never intended to be a democracy. Article IV, Section 4 of the U.S. Constitution says, in part, "The United States shall guarantee to every State in the Union a Republican form of Government...." The term "republican" in our constitution does not refer to the Republican Party because at the time the constitution was written, the Republican Party did not exist. If you have said the pledge of allegiance lately, you may have noticed the words: "I pledge allegiance to the Flag of the United States of America, and to the Republic for which it stands...." The United States is not a democracy. It is a republic—a government of law, not men.

Like so many elements of our federal government, the Electoral College was born of compromise. Why do we have a House and Senate in Congress? Compromise. The states with sparse populations wanted every state to have the same number of representatives. States with large populations wanted representation apportioned according to population. In the House, states are represented by population, and in the Senate, states have an equal number of votes—two.

The United States is one nation composed of many states. The principle of federalism, established since our beginning, places on individual states the majority of the burden for making decisions about elections, voter registration, and creating voting districts. States are composed of counties, and the counties have tremendous control over the nuts and bolts operations of elections.

If George W. Bush wins the presidency in the Electoral College but loses the popular vote, he will not be the first president who lost in popular vote, but still became President. In 1888, Grover Cleveland received 5,540,050 popular votes to 5,444,337 for Benjamin Harrison. However, Harrison received 233 electoral votes, while Cleveland received only 168. Harrison became the President.

Critics of the Electoral College talk about "fairness." Is it fair for the person who wins the popular vote to lose the election? If we lived in a democracy, the obvious answer would be "no." However, we live in a republic. In our republic, the rule of law dictates that the President of the United States must receive a majority of the electoral vote. It has been that way since the adoption of our constitution in 1789, with only slight modification.

Every time a cry issues forth to abolish or reform the Electoral College, that cry seems to fall on deaf ears. Why? Because, even though the Electoral College can produce some strange results at times, that institution is the best way to ensure that a balance between the will of the people and the will of the states prevails. The Electoral College ensures a balance between rural and urban interests, among regional interests, and between populous states and those states with small populations. Even Wyoming, population 453,588 according to the 1990 census, receives due consideration in hotly contested races. After all, Wyoming has three electoral votes, an electoral strength that belies its small population. Other states that fall into the three-vote category are Alaska, Delaware, Montana, North Dakota, South Dakota, and Vermont. In an election based strictly on popular vote, one good-sized city would cancel the votes of all these states put other.

The Electoral College has its beauty—the beauty of balance. We need to recognize both its beauty and genius.

Oh, it's CENU time again...

In 1787, while the United States Constitution was still being hotly debated in the fledgling states forming themselves into the United States of America, the Constitution required that "within three years" from that year, beginning in 1790, all the people of this nation would be counted every 10 years. In this present year the U.S. government will conduct Census 2000—the 22nd census.

In 1787, those who hammered out the Constitution assigned states one member of the House of Representatives for every 30,000 residents of their state—sort of. They calculated the number of residents of each state with this formula: the number of free persons plus those bound in servitude for a term of years (indentured servants) plus three-fifths of all other persons (slaves). Those who designed the document also decreed that "Indians not taxed" would be excluded from the census.

The purpose of the census was to establish proper representation in the U.S. House of Representatives. No state would have less than one representative, regardless of population. "Rhode-Island and Providence Plantations," our present state of Rhode Island, had one representative despite its small population. Had we maintained the one representative for each 30,000 people ratio, today's House of Representatives would have more than 9,000 members. At some point in history, the number of House members became fixed and House districts were realigned every 10 years to make sure that each House member represents about the same number of people.

Now, I have a reason for sharing this history lesson. If you read the U.S. Census Bureau's information on line, you will be hard pressed to discover the true purpose of the census. For instance, on the second page of the document titled "How America Knows What America Needs!" the census bureau provides uses of census information. In the section "Your Answers Work for You," the first reason listed to encourage people to fill out those forms says, "The federal government uses census numbers to allocate over $100 billion in federal funds annually for community programs and services, including education, housing and community development, health-care services for the elderly, job training and many more." The estimated figure for 2000 is actually $182 billion. In other words, be sure to fill out your census form and your area may win big bucks. Census answers equal $$$$$.

Reason two: State, local and tribal governments use census information for planning and allocating funds. So, once again, census answers equal $$$$$.

Reason three: Community organizations use census information to develop programs and services. Census answers equal allocation of $$$$$.

Reason four: businesses use census numbers to decide where to locate factories, shopping centers, movie theaters, banks, offices—"leading to the creation of jobs in your area." Census answers equals $$$$$.

Reason five: "The U.S. Congress uses the census totals to determine how many seats your state will have in the U.S.

House of Representatives. Likewise, states use the numbers to allocate seats in their legislatures."

I wonder why the real reason we even have the census is listed last. Could it be because the big, intrusive federal government feels the need to appeal to greed in order to garner accurate census data? Has the census become the latest version of "dialing for dollars"?

And what exactly do census takers need in order to perform their constitutionally mandated job? Well, unless I am missing something, the census bureau needs to know how many people live in your house...and who they are. For years and years, the census records included the names and ages of each person living in a household. Census records have been a goldmine for genealogical researchers. I doubt that future generations will be able to use our records. After all, laws protect the privacy of our census data.

So the census, designed by the framers of our Constitution as the mechanism for determining representation in the U.S. House, is now the tool of social planners who hold the strings to the federal purse.

I guess we should spell census a new way: CENU.

By the way—just where do "federal dollars" come from?

POW says faith helped him survive

When Kinston native son Eugene McDaniel returns home, he always receives an invitation to speak. His hair, grayer now than when its color gave him his nickname "Red," has thinned, but when he stands to his full 6-foot, 3-inch height, his presence is just as commanding as the day he climbed into his Navy A-6 to fly his 81st combat mission over North Vietnam.

That mission called for an Alpha Strike—an attack that would take McDaniel and his fellow Navy pilots into the heart of Hanoi. Their target was a key truck repair center just south of Hanoi at Van Dien. After completing his 80 previous missions, he had returned to base.

The 81st held something different. The fifth surface-to-air missile fired at his plane struck him aft. He and his bombardier-navigator, Lt. James Kelly Patterson, decided to try to nurse the wounded jet to a jungle mountain range before ejecting from the burning aircraft. Their chances for evading capture would be better in the mountains, McDaniel told Patterson. Both men ejected. The next day, McDaniel became a prisoner of war and Lt. Johnson became "missing in action." After more than six years of deprivation and torture, McDaniel finally was freed and returned home. Johnson is still MIA.

Capt. Red McDaniel did not spend his time Thursday morning talking about what he suffered as a POW. Instead, he told those who gathered at King's Restaurant to attend "The Second Annual National Day of Prayer Breakfast" about the courage and faith of the men who endured the perils of being treated as "war criminals" at the hands of one of history's most ruthless groups of captors.

"You can't put your faith in Wall Street," he told the group. "You can't put your faith in the Pentagon. The only thing you can put your trust in is the Lord." He quoted part of Romans 8:28: "And we know that all things work together for good to those that love God...." He emphasized the idea of "all things" by including his captivity and years as a prisoner of war, as well as the Sept. 11 attacks on America. He was able to find hope in the midst of hopelessness, goodness in the face of destruction.

"What happens to us is not nearly as important as how we react to it," he said. "Without faith, the journey through problems can become impossible."

He told how the men at the Hanoi Hilton developed ways to communicate in the midst of a news vacuum. They had no access to television, to radio, to newspapers or magazines. The only Bible verses they had were the ones they carried in their heads. Yet, these men worshipped regularly. They created an information network so all the men felt a part of the whole. Their communication system prevented the feelings of isolation that turn into despair.

"Faith is the substance of things hoped for, the evidence

of things not seen," McDaniel quoted from Hebrews 11. He explained that hope of release and hope of home helped the imprisoned men endure the torture, bear the years of confinement.

McDaniel told his listeners that the Sept. 11 attacks have forced America to reexamine its value system, to take stock of our personal and national values.

Then this former prisoner of war—recipient of the Navy Cross, two silver stars and three bronze stars—made a statement I don't think I'll ever forget:

"Courage is not the absence of fear. Courage is the presence of faith."

Whenever I think of courage, I'll remember these words and think of the tall man with thinning gray hair that everyone still calls "Red." I'll recall the man who did not maximize what he suffered but emphasized instead the faith in God that brought him through—and brought him home.

CHAPTER EIGHT

ODDS AND ENDS

'And it makes me wonder'

I don't know if I am just getting old and crotchety or if I've just started noticing more as my muffled heartbeats bring me closer to that cold hole in the ground. Take light bulbs, for instance. When I first moved into my house in 1973, the light bulbs we installed seemed to last for years. I don't think I changed my first light bulb here until 1983. Have the quality of light bulbs deteriorated like the quality of American-made cars did in the 1970's? I can scarcely enter a room in my house and flip a light switch without seeing a flash—and then darkness. I know I have changed the light bulb in our kitchen every other week for the past two years. Just when Sandra takes a notion to cook—which happens about every two weeks—she throws the switch and then calls out:

"Honey, the light bulb just blew. Can you change it?"

At the Parker manor, changing light bulbs is on my permanent "To Do" list. I have also noticed that when I need a 60-watt bulb, I either have a four-pack of 40's or a couple of 75's. Why do I even buy 40 watt and 75 watt bulbs when 99.9 percent of the time I need a 60?

A friend was leaving my house the other night. As I showed him to the door, I flipped on the porch light. Flash, pop—and darkness.

"Did you take my picture?" my friend asked.

"Of course not," I replied to my antsy friend. "The light bulb just blew."

"Looked like a photo flash to me," he said suspiciously. Come to think of it, that friend hasn't been back for about two months. He probably still thinks I snapped a quick picture. But why would I want a picture of him walking to his car?

Toilet paper is another cause for thought. How many sheets are they putting on a roll now? In the 1970's, we only had to replace the little cardboard empty every month or two. Then we had kids—1972, 1974, 1976 and 1981. As they got older, toilet paper started disappearing like fried chicken at a preachers' fellowship meeting. Of course, a couple of times, I entered the bathroom to find that a three-year-old had dropped a whole roll in the toilet.

"Don't you dare flush that toilet or you won't get an allowance until you turn 18," I'd yell at the offender.

"What's an allowance, Daddy?" my little blue-eyed cherub would ask.

"Well,...ugh...you'll understand it when you get older," I'd sputter.

"When I get old enough to understand where babies come from?"

"Maybe even a little older than that," I'd say.

Anyway, I have tried to read the stated number of "sheets" in a roll only to find myself needing a calculator to convert single-ply into double-ply in order to ascertain the real difference between a single roll, double roll and triple roll. I have come to one conclusion: a single roll, double roll and triple roll all magically disappear in the same limited amount of time. At my house now, that time span is about a day and a half.

Face it. Toilet paper is one of life's necessities—especially since I discovered the septic tank just won't process those Sears and Roebuck catalog pages. I started buying a four-roll pack, but soon moved to a six-roller as soon as the girls hit their pre-teens. Next, I went to 12-roll packs. The last two times I bought

TP, I purchased 24 packages. I guess the next step is to have a truckload delivered to the house.

Maybe I should just buy the stuff by the ton.

Then again, maybe I should buy some stock. Hmmm....

Those interstate flat tire blues

For the past few summers, my family made a grand swing north into Ohio and then back through Virginia. My mom and dad live in Ohio, just outside Columbus. My aunts, Judy and Dot, and a number of cousins live in Vinton, Virginia, just outside Roanoke. My brother, John, and his family also meet us in Vinton. After this family reunion, John's family and mine usually spend a couple of days visiting some historic sights. Last year we went to Williamsburg and Jamestown. This year we visited Richmond and Fredericksburg.

The first leg of the trip, to Ohio, was uneventful enough. Then we left Mom's and Dad's to head toward Vinton. We seemed to be cruising along at a good clip. I am an interstate driver. Interstates allow me to set the cruise and rack up the miles. Our normal route follows I-70 East to Cambridge, Ohio; then I-77 South to Princeton, West Virginia. Then we leave to interstate on U.S. 460 to Roanoke.

On this trip, about three miles north of Charleston, I heard a funny sound. Since the pavement is grooved at points around Charleston, I thought my tires on the pavement were causing the funny noise. Of course, traveling at 65 miles per hours means covering 95 feet each second—the length of a football field in a little more than three seconds. Just to be safe, I decided to pull to the side and check things out. I cut the radio off, killed the fan on the air conditioner, and gunned the engine. Everything sounded fine. Then I stepped out the car. The rear tire on the driver's side was flat. I got back in the car and moved it closer to the guardrail, turned off the engine, and set the brake.

Then I opened the trunk. I had forgotten that before I

could change the tire, I first had to unpack. Suitcases, a guitar, 4 million boxes of Jell-O gelatin and pudding that Sandra bought in Ohio, a case of applesauce, books, a camera bag—I stacked it all along the guard rail so I could access the spare, jack and tire tools. I tried to keep what I was thinking in my head and what I was muttering buried beneath my breath.

I removed the jack, but I didn't see the tire tools. Were we going to be stuck along the side of the road outside Charleston unable to change that tire? When I began to loosen the bolt securing the "doughnut," I saw a black package—the tire tools. As I placed the jack beneath the car, I realized just how hot it was outside the comfortably air-conditioned passenger compartment. The heat beat down from the sun and radiated up from the pavement. The more I cranked the car upward, the wetter my shirt grew. By the time I removed the flat tire and positioned the doughnut, sweat rolled down my backbone into my shorts. I tightened the lug nuts and stepped back.

"Have you got that spare on right?" Sandra asked.

"I think so, but I'd better check the manual."

I had put the doughnut on backwards.

Okay, so I'm not a mechanic. My dad always said, "Son, put that screw driver down—you don't know nothing about operating heavy equipment!" At least the car was still on the jack. I loosened the lugs, turned the spare around, and retightened the nuts. Since the tire I removed was much bigger than the doughnut, when I placed the flat in the trunk, I realized I had another problem. How on earth could I squeeze all that junk along the guardrail into my car. I loaded the trunk as best I could. Then Michael and I loaded the back seat. Finally, he squeezed his backsides into the narrow eight inches of seat left. Sandra, who was transporting purple passion plant from my mom and dad, looked like she was planted among objects surrounding her in the front seat. We were a rolling garden and junkyard combined.

Fortunately, just a few miles down the road, we found Mickey's Tire dealership. Someone other than Mickey told me the old tire was ruined, and he readily replaced it with a pricey brand-spanking new Michelin. He no doubt saw the license plate on my car and decided I would not likely be a repeat customer. Still, we were in and out in about 90 minutes, which afforded us time to eat lunch at a hot dog joint across the parking lot from Mickey's and take a little break.

We replaced the jack, tire tools and doughnut, repacked the trunk, and soon whizzed down the West Virginia Turnpike toward Princeton and our connection with U.S. 460 East to Roanoke. As I drove, I rejoiced about jacks, tire tools, spare "doughnuts" that work, and Mickey the tire dealer.

Life's little aggravations

Usually, I don't complain. My dad used to tell me that complaining is a waste of time because: 1) nobody wants to hear it, and 2) complaining alone almost never changes anything. As usual, Dad was right on target. But some practices in our society are so odious that they merit a few disparaging remarks.

The person, or people, who invented these recorded telephone menus must be on their way to the seventh ring of Dante's Inferno. You know the drill. I need to make a call to a business at the exact moment my time is worth about 50 bucks a minute. In my haste to make that call, I misdial at least twice, label myself an idiot, and finally punch in the right numbers.

"You have reached the offices of ABC Dealers," a recorded voice whines. "Please listen to the complete menu before keying your response. For the sales department, press one. For the credit department, press two. For the billing department, press three. To hear the menu of options again, press pound two, star four, star five, pound star one star pound. To talk to a real live person, hang up, get into your car, and drive to one of our convenient locations."

I press one. Then the voice starts intoning again.

"For sales—accounts receivable, please press one. For sales—customer service, press two. For sales—product information, press three. For sales—product liability information, press (mumble)."

I don't press a key, hoping against hope that if I hang on long enough, a living person will snatch up the phone and say: "Hey, Dumbo, why didn't you key in a number? What the heck do you want anyway?"

What happened to the days of a sweet voice answering the phone with: "Good morning. ABC Dealers. Mary Jo speaking. How may I direct your call?" Do business owners have any idea just how many times people call their businesses, confront that recorded labyrinth, and just hang up? Maybe they should have a "This line has been hit 1,325,276 times" like some web pages have. Business owners need a way to compare calls put through to calls attempted. Such numbers would give them an idea of how many times people decide that they won't play the maze game in order to earn an opportunity to give that business some of their money.

Two other pet peeves also have to do with telephone use, but I must admit that I am guilty of both sins. First, I hate talking to an answering machine. "At the sound of the tone, please leave your name, number, and a brief message." If the number of hang-ups I get on my answering machine is any indicator, I am not alone in declining to converse with a machine.

The second peeve is "call waiting." I call a friend and then next thing I know, the person tells me, "I just got beeped." Now I am drifting in phone company limbo. When I am talking to someone with some courtesy, in a few seconds, the person I called comes back on line. If the person I called has an advanced degree in rudeness, then I wait until the level of insult rises to "intolerable"—and hang up.

I added "call waiting" to my phone options when I had teen-age girls at home. My friends complained that I stayed on the phone so long they could never get a call through. I tried to explain that I was not on the phone—that one of my kids was. But their mentality was—hey, it's your phone, your number, so if I called your line and it was busy, you were the one talking.

Sometimes I long for simpler times—times before answering machines, before calling waiting beeps, and before recorded menus. But those times are as far removed from our lives as ancient Greece.

I wonder if I can create a recorded menu for my answering machine that could communicate with other recorded menus? Now, that's worth a thought.

Doing the Christmas hustle

Thursday morning at 6:50 am, more than 300 shoppers stretched before me as we waited for the Big K store in Reynoldsburg, Ohio, to open. I had arrived early because I had a mission to accomplish. Mom had charged me with seeking out some flannel shirts with Sherpa linings. These shirts are regularly priced between $17.99 and $19.99, but on sale for one day at Big K for $12.99, she explained.

The shirts were for Dad, who suffers constant chill. Mom usually stays at the other end of the thermonuclear spectrum. I knew Dad and I would have a busy day preparing the turkey for Thanksgiving dinner while Mom was at work, so I wanted to complete my task early and spend the rest of the morning drinking coffee with Dad and waiting for the arrival of granddaughter Courtney, daughter Sara and son-in-law Mark. (And we had to cook the turkey, too.)

So that's how I came to be standing outside Big K before 7 am on Thanksgiving Day as this year's edition of the Christmas hustle started. I use the term "Christmas hustle" as a double-edged sword. First, most of us have to hustle to get the shopping done before Santa makes his famous ride. Second, most of us try to keep from getting hustled by the merchants who do 25 percent of their business in the 30-day period from Thanksgiving to Christmas. And just how much shopping is that? Well, in raw numbers, this year Americans will spend an estimated $180 billion for Christmas presents—in retail stores. Those who surf the Net will spend another $6 billion. Grand total: $186 billion.

Break that down, news reports say, and we find that the typical family will spend an average of $825 for Christmas.

Eight hundred twenty-five dollars. Now, I don't know what that figure looks like where you sit, but $825 is a lot of money. For some folks, it's an entire week's pay. For others, it's two weeks pay...or even a month's pay.

"T'is the season to be afflicted by consumption craziness. Tra la la la la...la la la la." Now, before I am accused of spouting "Bah! Humbug!" let me assure you that my family does modest Christmas shopping and we try to give each other thoughtful gifts. I am not trying to rain on anybody's Christmas parade. But $825?

I have a suggestion. How about instead of spending the average, let's spend $725 on presents and give the other $100 to the Red Cross or some other charity of your choice. Can you imagine what we could do to relieve suffering if all of us made a donation of that size to disaster relief?

I see a more basic question. What is Christmas about, anyway? Is it just a time for conspicuous consumption, a time that we crowd each other's lives with more things we really don't need? We could all do with less getting and more giving.

The real Christmas present is the Lord Jesus. "For God so loved the world that he gave his only begotten son," John tells us in his gospel. This "only begotten son" came to teach us how to give—not gifts of material things, but gifts of love, compassion, time, energy—how to give ourselves. Yet, we have turned the season's message of giving intangibles into a time of mind-numbing buying.

Why not take a portion of what you plan to spend on Christmas and do something really selfless and beautiful with it? Explain what you are doing to your children...and explain why you are doing it. You may be surprised to see them learning the true lesson of Christmas.

Building a case against obesity

I am contemplating filing a lawsuit before long. I figure that the strategy worked against the tobacco industry, so it might just work for me. At issue is recent evidence that obesity is now at epidemic proportions. Jeffrey Koplan, director for the Centers for Disease Control, says: "Obesity contributes to about 300,000 deaths a year. It's probably only exceeded by smoking in contribution to death."

More than half of us—55 percent—weigh too much. The percentage of people who are obese—defined as those who weigh 30 pounds or more than they should—increased from 12 percent in 1991 to 17.9 percent in 1998. Why, that's nearly a six percent hike. If that rate of increase continues, by 2005 one in four Americans will be 30 pounds or more overweight.

Actually, today's figures are probably understated since many people fudge on their weight and height. We tend to understate weight and overstate height, so if someone tells you he weighs 255 pounds and is six feet tall, he probably weighs 270 pounds and is no more than 5 feet, 11 inches. Obesity is a serious national health problem that costs us billions of dollars in health care expenses and taxes to fund public health care programs. Researchers found that obesity is increasing in every race, every age group, and in both sexes.

Now, this is my plan. We need to file a class action suit against those who manufacture the food we eat. We could sue restaurants, fast food establishments, canneries, frozen dinner makers—the list is nearly endless. We don't really need to sue farmers because the tobacco settlement, hurricanes and floods have put most of them on the brink of extinction anyway.

Before you cast aside this idea, just think: Since the 1960s cigarette packs had government warnings about the dangers of smoking. Yet, Big Tobacco was found guilty of making a defective product and forced to cough up billions of dollars. Have you ever seen a warning on a Big Mac, Whopper, or Star burger? How about a warning on those cans of beans, that package of hotdogs, or that slab of bacon?

In fact, food advertisement rarely encourages us to eat healthy, eat responsibly, or eat in moderation. You are sitting in the privacy of your own home when—BAM—a commercial entices you to eat the latest fat-ladened, calorie-rich concoction.

No disclaimer appears to warn you that excessive eating can cause heart disease, high cholesterol, high blood pressure—not to mention high weight. No small print proclaims, "Doctors recommend that you eat a balanced diet which contains only moderate amounts of fat and sugars." Just as surely as Joe Camel helped lead innocents down the road to emphysema, these ads combine to take perfectly normal people and turn them into blubbery blobs lacking in energy and fitness.

For those of you who argue that obesity is genetic, please be advised that Koplan and William Dietz wrote in an editorial appearing in the Journal of the American Medical Association that "genes related to obesity are clearly not responsible for the epidemic of obesity because the gene pool in the United States did not change significantly between 1980 and 1994," according to an article published in the USA Today.

Well, I am certainly not responsible for my condition any more than smokers are responsible for getting hooked on smoking. The culprits must be those who produce and heavily advertise the foods we eat that make us into what we are. I think I'll look for a lawyer who will take my case on consignment. I figure both of us will make millions—maybe billions.

Maybe then I can find the time to exercise and eat right— and turn off the TV—in my personal battle against obesity.

Essential southern summer tips

Ever year when the heat of summer starts increasing from "simmer" to "bake" to "sear," we are bombarded with tons of tips for the summer. Wear loose fitting clothes. Wear a hat. Drink plenty of fluids. Know the difference between symptoms of heat exhaustion and heat stroke. Now, all these tips are important, and you need to keep them in mind. But after living in North Carolina for five to 10 years, most folks can quote these tips like a mantra. After all, surviving the "dog days" demands that we have a little fox bred into us.

But what about real issues? No one seems to be giving

important tips that touch us in those deepest hollows where we live. Okay, so we don't have any hollows around here. How about in the deepest furrows where we live?

Case in point: Don't order ice cream at the Dairy Queen and then head to your car. I forgot this important tip the other day. I walked into the Dairy Queen in Greenville, ordered a small dipped cone, and then hit the heat. Do you have any idea how fast that chocolate will melt and run down your hand as you try to unlock the car? And I have keyless entry.

Getting in the car does not solve the problem because if the outside temperature is 88, and the afternoon sun is bearing down, then your car has changed from "automobile" to "1500-watt microwave oven set on high." Chocolate that only trickled while I was outside began streaming once I entered the car. I was trying to move into the seat and hook the seat belt while lapping that ice cream cone like a thirsty hound dog. Listen, I can barely walk and rub my nose at the same time.

When I finally got the seat belt secured, I realized I had forgotten another important summer tip: start the car and let it run at least five minutes before touching the steering wheel. What is a steering wheel made of? The one in my car must have a plutonium core that melts down in summer sunlight. I reached for the wheel and was greeted by the sizzle of my fingertips. At least the FBI will never be able to use the fingerprints it has on file against me. I left my fingerprints—plus the other layers of my skin—on the surface of the wheel.

Cars sold in the South need a new option—the ever-cool steering wheel. I have never frozen my hands in the winter on the wheel, but I have baked and broiled them many-a time during the heat of summer. Sandra, my wife, keeps a white towel over her steering wheel to reduce the temperature of her auto-microwave from high to medium.

Child safety seats suffer from the same type of superheating. Grandchildren Courtney and Haley visited with us during parts of the Third and Fourth of July. Time came for Sandra to take them home.

"Honey, would you put the car seats in my car?" she asked in her most syrupy voice—a voice that I am not accustomed to hearing and that always shocks me into immediate action.

"Sure," I said, already moving. "Glad to." Then I realized that she had pulled a "gotcha." Either consciously or subconsciously she understood that the inside temperature of her car would be at least 180 degrees. She also knows that when I install the seats in her little two-door Accent, I must move the front seats all the way forward, climb in, and face the back. Facing to the rear allows me to thread the seat belt through the child seats and press on them to secure them properly. When it comes to safety seat stability for my grandchildren, no NASA astronaut has ever been held more securely in place.

I took Haley's car seat from the house and installed it. In the process, I happened to grab the exposed metal end of the seat belt—only briefly. Did the pain jolt me? Nah, just don't take me long to examine a seat belt end. When Haley's seat was fastened in, I went to my car to remove Courtney's seat. I hit the release, grabbed the seat, and was immediately reminded of an Old Testament verse: "Thou shalt not let thy seed pass through the fires of Moloch." Hand repositioned, I quickly installed Courtney's seat.

By this time, I was trying to recall the symptoms of heat exhaustion versus heat stroke. My shirt looked like I had played—and lost—a best-of-five-set tennis match. The heat continued to hiss at me through the windshield. How could I sacrifice my little granddaughters to Moloch of the South? I started the car, turned the air conditioner to its most friendly position, and went in the house.

"Get the car seats in, honey?" Sandra asked in her best butter-won't melt-in-my-mouth tone. But I barely heard her. I was busy searching for the first aid booklet to brush up on heat stroke and heat exhaustion.

"Honey, do you know where we keep the first-aid cream?" I called out.

Cyberspace folklore

Poor little Amy Bruce. The verbally precocious 7-year-old abuse victim has a brain tumor, and the Make-A-Wish Foundation is going to do something special for her if she can just get enough folks to forward her story via email. And Kelsey Brooke Jones' story still is making the rounds. For those of you on the Internet who haven't heard, little Kelsey is missing, and has been now for about six months. The email includes a color photo and asks recipients to forward the message to everyone.

Gerber Foods, in a settlement resulting from a class action suit, must give every child in the United States born between 1985 and 1997 a $500 savings bond.

Amy, Kelsey and the Gerber Food settlement are just the latest in the never-ending list of Internet hoaxes, legends and rumors speeding their way to our email boxes. Amy does not exist. The real Kelsey Jones was missing only two hours. And Gerber is not giving away savings bonds.

I receive from six to a dozen of these messages every week. Misinformation at the speed of light—or at least at 56K per second.

My daughter Rachel recently wrote me with two inquiries. One said that people who used antiperspirants instead of deodorants are setting themselves up to develop breast cancer. The message urged the recipients to forward this important message to everyone they love. Rachel had checked the message and already knew it was bogus.

Then, she mentioned another message that told her how to do CPR on herself. Just place that one in the file alongside the infamous stories of the "butt spider," the Inside Edition mall abduction warnings, the dreaded cancer-causing sodium laureth sulfate in your shampoo, and the rest.

After I received the Amy Bruce email three times this week, I found a copy that had an actual phone number—an employee in the business office of Case Western Reserve

University. The tag information included a phone number, so I dialed to see if the phone number was legit.

Helen answered the phone. When I told her the purpose of the call, she said:

"It's a hoax. I don't know how my name got on that thing, but since it has, I have been receiving hundreds of calls. It has been a nightmare."

I constantly respond to those who send me these urban legends, hoaxes and rumors. I urge them to stop hitting the "forward" button that launches the next salvo of misinformation. I refer them to websites where they can go to verify the stories before they send a spurious message to another 20 or 30 people.

And still these messages come.

So, I beg you. Before you alarm your loved ones about the "butt spider" or the perils of antiperspirants, before you send the emails that beg you to "forward this message to everyone on your list," before you keep the legends and hoaxes alive and clog the Internet with false information—check it out.

Go to http:\\www.hoaxkill.com or http:\\www.urbanlegen ds.about.com and check the legitimacy of these messages.

We are tendered-hearted people, so we enlist the support of our friends in response to letters that plead for us to help sick and dying children such as Amy, or Jessica Mydek or David Lawitts, or Tamara Martin or Timothy Flyte—even though all these letters are hoaxes. We are fearful people, scared to death of the real devastations of cancer—so we forward false warnings about antiperspirants or aspartame or shampoos with supposed carcinogens.

We end up being the dupes of those who know how to tug at our hearts, or play to our fears or greed. But no matter how many times a spurious email makes the Internet rounds, Bill Gates is not going to give you $1,000 or a trip to Disney World, Abercrombie and Fitch or the Gap will not send you free clothing, IBM will not give you a free computer.

So before forwarding a message, try to verify it. No use spreading false alarm, false hope or false information, is there?

Rain can't dampen Relay for Life 2000

Dark rain clouds threatened and lower-than-normal temperatures gave the damp air a little extra bite, but sunny expressions and hopeful attitudes marked the true spirit of this weekend's Relay for Life. Dozens of cancer survivors and dozens of Relay teams squeezed into the North Lenoir High School cafeteria for the opening exercises.

"We just sent the fire marshal to dinner," quipped Principal Doyle Brinson as he surveyed the sea of folks occupying nearly every square foot of floor space and crowding the area just outside the cafeteria proper.

I didn't get a program. In fact, I saw only one and never had a chance to peek at it, so I can't give all the names of those who spoke during the opening exercises. Frankly, some folks were in so much rain gear and jungle hats, I wouldn't have recognized them at that distance anyway. I know Channel 12's Skip Waters was running late. He made a dash from New Bern after finishing Friday evening's weather forecast.

But I guarantee you that not one of them will care whether or not they receive a public mention here because no one in that cafeteria came for recognition. Instead, they were present as part of Lenoir County's team against cancer in all its ugly forms. I am ashamed to admit that Friday evening was the first time I attended any part of this county's Relay for Life. I found out something as I sat in the cafeteria. Two banners hanging on the wall caught my attention. One said, "Top 10 Nationwide / Relay for Life Community / 1998." The other said, "Top 10 Nationwide / Relay for Life Community / 1999."

Top 10 nationwide?

Paul Rodgman stepped to the microphone. Until the survivor's reception earlier that evening, I never even knew Paul had battled cancer. He is a two-year survivor. He looked into that sea of faces and said, "All of us are walking together toward a goal—to eliminate cancer." He reminded the group that surviving cancer demands more than good luck...it demands research into new technologies and treatments.

Paul recognized his son, his daughter, and his wife. My vision blurred. You see, his wife, Ella, became involved in Lenoir County's Relay for Life in 1997—before Paul was diagnosed. Later that same year, Paul went for a routine checkup and his doctor found the cancer lurking within. He briefly described his treatments.

"My wife, my son, my daughter and I went through it as a team—and that's what you'll hear from all these survivors," he said.

How true, I thought. For, you see, Team Parker went through its own battle against cancer. Sandra, Michael, Sara, Rachel, Lydia and I know the pangs of uncertainty, the rigors of treatment, the discouragement of side effects and fatigue, and the numbness of mind a cancer victim and his or her support team endures. Sandra is a two-year survivor. Her cancer was an aggressive one. Ten to 15 years ago, only two percent of women with her type of cancer survived passed five years. By the time she was diagnosed in 1998, that figure was up to 40 percent.

But dramatic improvement in the odds of surviving cancer comes at a cost. Friday night 42 teams, composed of anywhere from 10 to 40 people, helped pay part of that cost by walking throughout the night and most of the next day to raise the money needed for research.

Over the past three years, Lenoir County's Relay for Life has raised more than $300,000 toward that battle. Last year, the Relay for Life efforts across this state raised $3 million, and $4 million flowed back in the form of research grants to our state's four medical schools. More research translates into better odds for cancer's victims. More research means we come closer to winning the war against this disease in all its hideous manifestations.

As part of the opening exercise, survivors stepped to the microphone one at a time to give name, type of cancer, and length of survival. Of those who stepped up, some were children, and some were great-grandparents. Some had only started their battle for survival and counted their time in months, not years. But a number of survivors have beaten the disease 10 years, 15 years, 20, years, 25 years. One woman stepped up and announced that she had been a survivor for 40 years.

For Paul and Sandra, the number is two years...and counting.

Non-traditional students a delight

I usually spend at least part of my weekends in a classroom at East Carolina University. Most folks know I have taught at East Carolina part-time for more than a decade. But for the past four years or so, I have been teaching in a special program at ECU called "Weekend University." The "Weekend University" program targets non-traditional students who want to attend college but cannot attend day classes—or even night classes. So, to meet their needs, East Carolina offers classes on Friday evenings and all day Saturdays.

"Non-traditional student" generally describes someone who cannot fit the regular university program into his or her life. In my experience, these students are adults, many approaching or well within middle age, who are seeking degrees as a way to make themselves more suited to management positions, who are trying to hone skills they already have, or who tried the college scene years ago as teens and found it easier to party than study.

Regardless of what twist of fate brings them to Weekend University, they tend to share some characteristics. Of course, since they have been out of school a decade or two, they enter the college classroom with uncertainty. In fact, some of them seem to bring tractor-trailer loads of self-doubt. But once they get a course or two behind them, they understand that they can learn, they can achieve, and they can excel.

One former student began his quest for a college degree at 57. Dwight is a successful manager who listened to the reasons he gave his daughter when he encouraged her to attend college—and then took his own advice. He is not looking for a degree as a ticket to a good job. He already has a good job that pays well. He is not looking at a degree as security for the future. His job is secure.

But he sold his daughter on the idea that getting an education enriches a person's life. His own argument convinced him that even though a degree will not translate into dollars, his life needed some enriching in other ways. He has taken two classes with me, and I still see him every Saturday as he takes other classes.

On Saturdays I see a couple from Havelock. Matt told me once that he was working on a degree to get a job that would mean a cut in pay. That was his way of saying that he, too, was learning for the sheer reward of learning.

Of course, I work with other students who hope to parlay their degrees into better jobs. But these students share something: they have gotten to a point in their lives where they value education. They come with a seriousness of purpose and a willingness to work uncommon in most teen college students. They also bring a great deal to the classroom—life experience, determination, knowledge of what real success in life is all about, and a thirst for learning.

Teaching them is more than a pleasure—it is a privilege.

So, for those of you who sometimes yearn to return to school, for those who want to earn that degree you just never had the opportunity to complete earlier in your life, for those who just want to learn for the sake of knowledge itself, "Weekend University" may be the vehicle to change your dream into a reality. You may even walk into a room in the General Classroom Building and see me at the board.

I'll be waiting.

Florida election enlightens nation

I have to be frank. After years of mundane presidential elections in which the networks called the winner before bedtime in Missouri, the drama of this year's presidential race was exciting—for a while. You remember. On election night, the networks called Florida for Gore and then later for Bush. After announcing George W. was the winner, Florida went gray again—too close to call.

Less than one-half of one percent of votes separated the two presidential hopefuls. In fact, according to the first unofficial official count, Bush won Florida's 25 electoral votes by 930 votes. But those certified results were in no way the official votes because for the first time in presidential history, absentee ballots could have changed the outcome.

Of course, these ballots haven't changed the outcome yet, and Broward and Palm Beach counties were still counting into the wee hours of Sunday morning and through most of the day Sunday, as election officials in these highly Democratic counties searched for enough Al Gore ballots to deliver Florida's electoral votes—and the Presidency—to the Vice Prez. Even when we think this election is finally over, the court battles will begin in earnest.

I know what you are thinking. You are tired of all this election news and analysis. So am I...except we should thank the folks in Florida for teaching us some new election terminology. This year, more than any other, all of us have received an intense civics lesson about how our presidential election system really works.

Take "chad," for instance. Until this election, I thought Chad was some guy's name or the name of an African nation. Now I know that a "chad" is a little piece of paper punched (or not punched) from a ballot. Ballot chads come in a variety of shapes and sizes. We have the clear punched chad. Actually, we don't have that chad because it dropped into the voting netherworld after the stylus poked it away.

Then we have the hanging chad—the bit of paper hanging by one or two or even three corners. The voting machines in Florida routinely toss these votes because the voting machines can count only chadless ballots. And don't forget the dreaded dimpled chad. A dimpled chad occurs when the stylus, for some reason, did not penetrate the ballot with sufficient force to clear the chad away or create a hanging chad. Voting machines despise dimples, so the machines kick out all dimpled ballots in disgust.

Voting machine rejection brings us to next term Florida has taught us—"voter intent." Now, as I understand it, in order to vote in any state but Florida, a registered voter must cast a properly marked ballot. If the ballot is not properly marked, then the vote does not count. But in Florida, election canvassers are required to do more. Canvassers are required to look at the ballot, see if a dimpled chad mars the ballot, magically ascertain what the voter intended to do—and then count the vote for Gore.

I saw this same scenario acted out Friday when East Carolina played Southern Mississippi in football. On the last play of the game, a Southern Miss receiver caught a pass and took two steps before a Pirate defender decked him. Time ran off the clock, and ECU's team left the field thinking they had won the game, 14-9. Officials huddled and invoked what will now be called the "Florida rule." The receiver, they reasoned, intended to drop that pass. An incomplete pass stops the clock. So the Hattiesburg homers decided to put two seconds back on the clock and allow Southern Miss one more play. Of course, Southern Miss still lost.

I understand that folks who play "Super Lotto" and "Powerball" now plan to invoke the "Florida rule."

"But I intended to pick the winning numbers," one player whined last Wednesday in Ohio's big game. "Florida rule." Now lotto officials in Ohio are huddling. Do they give the guy the $9 million or not?

If North Carolina students start using the "Florida rule," we may finally begin to see our SAT scores rise. After all, don't the students intend to pick the right answer?

I plan to use the new rule at tax time.

"You see, Mr. IRS agent, I intended to have enough deductions to offset any tax I owe. In fact, I intended to have enough deductions to receive a full tax refund for all the taxes I paid in 2000. Florida Rule!"

I'm already making plans on how to use this refund windfall.

Forget the hype — Get it right

Did you know that, according to a newspaper headline, a woman gave birth to twins—one in the last century and the other in this century? The broadcast media made the point even more strongly: she gave birth to her two children in different millennia.

Welcome to the new century...the new millennium. At least, that's what all the hype says, isn't it? Never mind all that. The hype is not true. And before you turn to something else, I promise I am not going to spend the space here explaining why the year 2000 is the last year of the 20th century and the last year of the second millennium. I've done that already. Besides, if you do not want to take my word for it, I'll refer you to this nation's official timekeeper: the United States Naval Observatory. You can access the website at http://psyche.usno.navy.mil/millennium/whenIs.html .

So what is the point? The point is that accuracy and truth no longer mean anything to national television networks and media conglomerates. As 1999 ticked away, all the networks had their folks primed to greet the new millennium—whether the new millennium came or not. Do NBC, ABC, CBS, Fox and the rest have less research resources than I have? Do you mean to tell me that among all these networks not one single person knows what I know? Not one can check the information even though the U.S. Naval Observatory has the facts posted on its website?

One columnist for the News and Observer called people like me "purists" and said that the reason they didn't raise a fight with us over the millennium issue is that they didn't dispute our claims—they just didn't care. Now, I don't have a problem with millions of people packing Times Square to celebrate as they watched a one and three nines turn into a two and three zeros. I enjoy watching the odometer on my car do the same thing. So if folks wanted to hoop and holler and spray each other with champagne, I don't mind. In the light of media-hyped predictions of Y2K disasters, the massive gathering of folks was like a testimony to their faith that the Y2K bug wouldn't bite.

But for the media to proclaim, nearly universally, the coming of a new century and a new millennium when the folks who work in the news organizations know full well that the hype was a blatant lie—now that bothers me. It smacks of an arrogance that says, "The facts are what we say they are."

People always cuss their hometown newspaper. Lewis Grizzard shared his response to those who asked him why his paper couldn't be more truthful and accurate.

"Man, the paper only costs 35 cents," Grizzard would say. "What do you want for a dime and a quarter? The truth? If you want the truth, that'll cost $3.95."

Truth. Accuracy. Are those characteristics really too much to ask?

Evidently.

"But," you might say, "this millennium hype is such a small thing."

Is it? We are not even talking about a close call on this issue. We are talking about blatant misrepresentation. We are talking about the national media that knowingly focused on a lie, confident that if the media hammered it enough, the people as a whole would believe it and buy into it.

Which they did.

Do we want them to take the same approach to election coverage? Trial coverage? Governmental reporting?

How do we know they don't?

Just who tried it first?

I sat in a training session at Lenoir Community College that focused on drug and alcohol abuse issues. The speaker, Steve Wilson of North Carolina's Employee Assistance Program, was informative and entertaining. During the course of the presentation, he raised this question: Who was the first person that flipped over a hardened cow pie, saw a mushroom growing beneath it, and decided, "Hey! That mushroom might be tasty?" I thought about his point. Who—exactly—would be that adventurous or, in my narrow mind, that stupid?

Since that presentation, I've thought about other issues and wondered who might be the first person to even think up some of the hare-brained ideas in current circulation. Take bungee jumping. I have a good selection of bungee straps. I've used them to hold my truck closed, to secure my son's bike to the rack on his car, and to wrap around suitcases that simply don't want to stay closed. Bungee straps are useful items.

However, at some point someone decided to tie together, say 15 or 20 or 50 feet of them, and then jump headfirst off a bridge or building. Just what brave soul risked such a stunt, secure in the belief that those bungee straps would support his or her weight and bring the jumper bouncing back?

How many people went "Wheeeee!" and then "Splat" to perfect the bungee jumping art? What kind of person decided that hanging upside down and doing the boing-boing bounce was actually fun? What is the world record for bungee jumping?

But bungee jumping pales beside other daredevil activities. Take cooking. How did someone decide that if raw meat and veggies tasted good, flame broiling would make them better? How many toasted tongues and fried fingers did it take for people to finally learn to control the Promethean gift?

Who was the first person to cook spaghetti? Now, I love spaghetti just as much as the next person, but I have to be frank—spaghetti looks a lot like long, thin, albino worms. I am sure that somewhere someone rolled a wad of pasta out into a worm-like string as a Halloween prank. This jokester wanted to create the appearance of worms in bloody sauce—and voila!—spaghetti was born.

Listen, someone had to be the first brave soul to try chitterlings. I can see eating the rump or shoulder of a pig—even the meaty ribs. But who in their right mind would unwind the intestines, get a whiff, and decide—"Hmmm! Smells like food"? Ever smell chitterlings cooking? They smell even worse than collards—and we all know what collards smell like when they cook. Swamp gas would be a refreshing fragrance by comparison. And pig's feet? Someone watched a hog walking around in the muck and mire and—well, other things—and started to salivate?

How many alternative daredevils failed to make the cut? Like the person who brewed toadstool soup? And the first connoisseur of poke-berry pie? How about the guy who tried shoestring jumping?

My son Michael recently revealed that when he was just a lad, he once jumped off our roof to prove that if he did a G.I. Joe tuck and roll upon landing, he would not be hurt. He made the jump and wasn't hurt. I sat in amazement as I listened to Michael recount this story. I kept asking myself, "What dark spasm of idiocy racked his brain before he pulled that stunt?" Probably the same spasm of idiocy that induce someone to kick over a cow patty, uncover a mushroom, and pop that mushroom a la cow dung into his mouth.

Well, I've about pondered these mysteries all I can for now. My head is hurting, and my heart is fluttering like I just dropped 150 feet to the end of a bunch of bungee straps.

One more thing: Who thought up the idea of a newspaper columnist stringing together a bunch of his pieces and calling them a book? We probably have Mark Twain to thank for that. Lewis Grizzard deserves a nod, as well.

Man, am I out of my league.